The UK Air Fryer Recipe Book

1200-Day Quick and Affordable Meals incl. Side Dishes, Desserts, Snacks, and More for Beginners and Advanced Users

Ruth E. Hill

Contents

Introduction

Air fryers have taken the mantle in our kitchen of late, and we cannot dispute their functionality. I have one in my kitchen, and it is pretty impressive as I can cook and preheat non-fuss and delicious recipes at home that are super cool. Currently, I enjoy being with family members at my apartment, mainly during the weekend, eating all kinds of fried foods made using the latest appliance, and it's entertaining to reckon.

Most individuals think that cooking foods using air fryers is less messy and healthy, which is true, but there is more than that. Air fryers are good at preparing crispy foods without tampering with their nutritional and tasty value. Essentially I research how food produced in the market or local supermarket can be cooked by checking their   I embark on using my air fryer. Doing so has helped me explore new ways of cook   such as French fries, chicken breasts, and cookies.

Also, cooking ideal recipes like desserts, snacks, fish, meat, and vegetables is what I love most because I read detailed recipes and keep implementing the practice. As such, owning an air fryer has become part of me in knowing a quality appliance that uses little oil, meaning achieving food with less cholesterol and low calories is possible. Since I love crispy and lip-smacking food, having an air fryer has quenched my thirst, which could not be attained, not to forget the yummy tasty food I get.

Unlike traditional ovens, air fryers are dishwasher safe, which eases their cleaning process. As a result, Air fryers improve the kitchen appeal and simplify how arrangements can be made without inconveniencing the users with messy and greasy coatings. This is why if you have craved classic fries without calories and oil, you can embrace using an air fryer at home. In addition, you can easily illuminate using an air fryer even though you may be a novice to safely roast, bake and steam a delicious meal of your choice.

Even though air fryers are perfect appliances, handling them poorly and improperly can damage them quickly. Appropriate cleaning and maintenance should be implemented to effectively protect their working conditions and operationality. The process can also improve your kitchen appeal to a more efficient arena suitable for cooking delicious foods with their actual nutritious value. Light cleaning the air fryer is the best alternative after use since it removes residues before they compact and hardens on the pan or basket surfaces.

In this cookbook, I will lay out the features of an air fryer, foods to cook and avoid in the air fryer, benefits of air fryer, maintenance of air fryer, and tips to consider when using an air fryer. So read this complete guide and get incredible insights on the fundamentals of an air fryer.

Getting to know the air fryer

Air fryers are equipped and designed with practical parts to streamline and ensure your cooking journey is seamless. They are also built with the latest vortex technology to bring outstanding user experiences when trying various dishes. Before using an air fryer, it is essential to understand the functionality and design

of each feature of the appliance to achieve the best performance and improve its efficacy and efficiency. Here are the typical features of an air fryer:

1.Air outlet openings

Air fryers have outlet openings to ensure ample airflow, thus preventing overheating in the device. This safety concern is essential in emitting hot air and passing in cool air for free circulation. It is usually located at the back of the device.

2.Air inlet

The Air inlet is found on the top of the device and maintains the natural air circulation around the air fryer. The air inlet optimizes the cooking process of the air fryer to be effective.

3.Air fryer drawer

Air fryers have drawers for covering and protecting the inner basket. The drawer also collects emitted oil coming from food ingredients. When shaking the basket, remove the container inside the drawer and stir as required.

4.Air fryer basket

The air fryer basket is the main component that holds food in the appliance. It has tiny heatproof holes that allow drops of grease into the drawer chamber and cooks crisper recipes.

5.Air fryer heating coil element

The heating coil element is a superb component that generates enormous temperatures, suitable for expediently preparing food. It is located under the fan, which blows hot air at a very high speed, taking less time to preheat even before cooking starts.

6.Fan

An air fryer fan is essential in providing good circulation of hot hair in the inner basket containing the food ingredients. It lies above the heating coil and dispenses hot air uniformly.

7.Advanced touchscreen

All air fryers of high quality are fitted with advanced touchscreens to ease the process of making delicious food. In addition, air fryers have cook time maintenance and control temperature systems that can be adjusted seamlessly.

8.Temperature control button

Advanced air fryers are designed and built with temperature settings to maintain specific food recipes' temperatures. The button typically differs according to the device; for instance, most small airtight devices let up to 200 degrees Celsius/400 degrees Fahrenheit.

9.Bumper Rubber

The air fryer's bumper rubber is a valuable accessory for protecting the bottom part from scratch. The rubber bumpers provide a minimal gap between the base and frying parts to prevent the device from melting, and it is usually made of silicone rubbers.

Food to cook in an air fryer and food to avoid

Air fryers can be versatile and convenient when cooking and preparing numerous dishes; however, not all foods can be tossed onto this kitchen appliance. Here is a list of the foods you can cook and avoid when using an air fryer according to renowned chefs and most culinary experts;

Foods to cook in an air fryer

1.Frozen food

An air fryer is an excellent alliance for cooking and reheating food that has been frozen. The appliance does a great job of ensuring the food gets crispy through its conventional feature that allows hot air to circulate freely and quickly in a precise manner.

2.Brussels sprouts

Brussels sprouts do magically well in an air fryer. It ensures the sprouts get super crispy, thus reducing the mess of dealing with the greasiness of oil.

3.Cookies

Cookies are best prepared using an air fryer since the appliance does not require preheating time. You can keep your cookie-dough balls in your hand freezer without making the entire batch and use the air fryer to make homemade cookies quickly.

4.Cooked steak

Because air fryers work like miniature ovens, they are good at cooking steak. Just by simple practice, you can essentially get an excellently cooked steak, making you avoid flames and smoke from the grill. In addition, it does not leave up the mess from searing steak and frees up the stovetop.

5. Chicken breasts

Unlike the stovetop or oven, an air fryer yields juicer chicken breasts. Air fryers have compact designs, ensuring there is no room for the evaporation of juices like other methods. The even flow of air in the air fryer ensures the chicken is caramelized and takes the roast chicken to another level. Avoid glazing on your chicken since the excess may spread and drip on the air fryer chamber.

6.Bacon

The best way to cook bacon is by using an air fryer. An air fryer ensures the fat drips from the basket leaner, thus reducing the greasy mess. It also involves minimum supervision, unlike using an oven or stovetop.

7.Zoodles

Zoodles can ideally be made from an air fryer. The food releases tons of moisture when cooking, which can help swiftly maximize drip outs in the basket, giving you perfect al dente zucchini noodles.

Foods to avoid using an air fryer

1.Whole chickens or large roasts

Whole chicken and large roasts will not cook well in an air fryer since they will not get an even hot air flow. The part close to the heat will burn and dry out before the parts far from the heat source become safe to eat.

2.Food with wet batter

You should avoid putting foods that contain wet natter in an air fryer, like tempura shrimp and corndogs. Wet batter revolves everywhere, and

without an appropriate oil bath, the batter will not set, thus making it not crispy. The batter will make the food drip off, thus burning and sticking on the bottom of the air fryer ending up chewy.

3.Cheese
You should avoid putting cheese in an air fryer as it can build an enormous mess in your air fryer. This is not an actual fryer you can use to deep fry mozzarella sticks or cheese because it can bring a cheesy mess.

4.Fresh greens
Fresh greens such as kale and spinach are food substances you should avoid putting in an air fryer. The greens will typically fly over and cook unevenly. If you want to cook fresh greens, stick to the standard ovens.

5.Medium rare burgers
Knowing that medium rare burgers cannot happen in an air fryer is normal. Re-burgers usually take a short time in an air fryer. Thus, it won't have a considerable time to be brown.

6.Vegetables and over-seasoned proteins
Over-seasoning your veggies and meat before putting them in an air fryer is a colossal mistake. Generally, having food with a dry surface due to seasoning can make them be blown by airflow in the air dryer or make them fall through the basket.

Benefits of air fryer
Air Fryer's trend is genuinely and reasonably at its prime since more and more people keep buying and realizing its usefulness. Owning an Air Fryer majorly differs from other cooking appliances that keep coming and going down in popularity which you can send goodwill after a year. Purchasing one of the air fryers is an intelligent decision you can make, and you will not regret it. Check the following exceptional benefits of owning an air fryer.

1.Safer, faster, and easier to use
Most individuals at home love to cook frequently but lack time to do so. That's why takeaway meals are top-rated currently, even though they are unhealthy. For instance, if you cook foods such as pork chops or salmon in less than 20 minutes, it is probable to order out than cook it.

Since air fryers are easy and fast, it uncomplicates the cooking process. You will only trim the pieces of food substances like meat and potatoes, then put them in the basket and set it out to cook.

2.A healthier way of coking
When purchasing an air fryer, most individuals consider the prospect of healthier cooking. With just little oil used in the cooking process, it is an excellent way of replacing deep-fried foods that are not very healthy with better alternatives.

You will spray fried foods such as fried fish and breaded chicken tenders with tiny bits of salt, and the breeding will get crispy as it cooks, thus using fewer oils. You can also cook tater tots and French fries and achieve crispy results without deep frying.

3.Air fryers are very versatile.
An air fryer is a healthier cooking alternative, unlike deep frying. Also, with an air fryer, you can virtually cook any food substance, like whole spaghetti squash, fried chicken, desserts, and curries. The air fryers are best for cooking frozen food substances bought in stores like pizza, French fries, and tater tots.

4.Air fryers reheat food more efficiently.

You cannot only cook food using an air fryer but rather use it to reheat ready food making it very useful. Air fryers ease the reheating process and ensure the food does not burn or overcook since they can automatically control its heating temperatures. In addition, air fryers keep the food fresh in taste and make the food crispy.

5.Faster as compared to oven cooking

The perfect part of an air fryer is that it gets hot quickly, with the circulating air helping the food to cook evenly, get crispy, and brown without additional interventions from the user, thus reducing your cooking time. Air fryers are smaller, unlike cooking ovens, which heat quickly and faster. Typically, an oven takes a preheat time of about 10 minutes, but for an air fryer, there is no preheating time for most food recipes.

All this means you can put the food in the basket, connect the air fryer, set the time, and wait 10-15 minutes for your food to be ready. An air fryer is an excellent appliance for easy and quick snacks, whether for a school retreat or an after-party event, as it can cook your snack to perfection in a super easy way just by turning the off and on buttons.

6.Very easy to clean

Who doesn't clean after cooking in the world? The truth deal is an air fryer can effectively erase the unpleasant task of wiping away in ensuring the pleasure of your meal is outstanding. As such, you will get to know that air fryers are incredibly easy to clean after being used.

Air fryers only require regular cleaning, like any pan or pot you use. You use a non-scratch sponge after adding soapy water to the basket to clean the interior and the exterior. Also, some air fryers are dishwasher safe.

Furthermore, ensure you deep clean the whole unit, including the coil, once or twice a month, according to your use level. If you probably clean often, it is not a tiresome process compared to an oven.

Cleaning and maintenance

Air fryers are superb appliances that are easy to use, very convenient, and good to cook, but they may not last long if proper cleaning and maintenance are not implemented. Ensure you keep the following guidelines to achieve the value of an air fryer and make the appliance productive for some years to come.

How to clean the air fryer

Essentially deep frying food is relatively messy and can make your pans dirty, give the fryer a greasy coating all around and make your utensils grimy. However, air fryers are relatively clean since the cooking basket is fully enclosed, thus eliminating splattering of grease, fat, and oil in all your food drips down into the pan. Therefore, ensure you clean your air fryer after every use by following the steps listed below:

- After using the air fryer, unplug it from the wall socket and leave it to cool down.
- Use a damp cloth to wipe the exterior parts.
- Wash the basket, pan, and tray using dishwashing soap and hot water. All components of the air fryer that are removable are dishwasher safe and, thus, can be put in a dishwasher if you consider not washing by hand.
- Clean inside the air fryer using a cloth or sponge and hot water
- Remove any food residue stuck on the heating element above the food basket using a brush
- Leave the basket, tray, and pan to dry out before placing them back onto the air fryer.

Essential Tips;
- If the food has stuck and hardened on the basket or pan, soak them with hot water and soap to soften the food to be easily removed.
- Do not use other utensils to remove food residue in the air fryer components. Air fryer components may have lined with a non-stick coating that is easy to remove; therefore, use a continually non-abrasive sponge to remove foodstuffs stuck on the drip pan or the basket.
- When cooking sequential batches of food, wait until the final batch is finalized to opt for cleaning the air fryer.

Storing the air fryer appropriately.

After the air fryer has been cleaned, ensure you store it safely. When storing it, ensure it is not plugged into a wall outlet and is standing in an upright position. If there are any storage compartments for cords, tuck the cords earlier to place the fryer away.

How to maintain the air fryer

Beyond frequent cleanings of your air fryer, there are basic maintenance requirements to implement to make it function correctly and ensure it is not damaged. These requirements include the following;
- Inspecting air fryer cords before every use. Never plug a frayed or damaged cord into an outlet since it can cause severe injuries and, in extreme cases, death. Ensure the cords are damage free and clean before using the appliance.
- Ensure the air fryer is positioned upright, on a flat surface, before you start your cooking process.
- Ensure the appliance is free of debris and clean before cooking. You may have left the air fryer for a long time without using it, so check inside if dust has accumulated or if there is any food residue in the basket before cooking.
- Visually check every component of the air fryer, be it the pan, basket, and handle, to ascertain their state to contact the manufacturer and get a replacement. Putting the air fryer in enclosed areas can make it overheat.
- Avoid placing the air fryer close to other appliances or the wall. Typically, air fryers can be placed at least 4 inches above and behind to sufficiently vent hot air and steam while cooking.

Tips and tricks for the air fryer

Besides crisping food without oil, an air fryer has a lot of uses. For instance, you can roast pork

or a whole chicken, dehydrate foods such as meats or fruits and reheat food quickly. An air fryer works like an oven by taking less time, getting the crispy food outside, and making it moist inside.

Since an air fryer is a helpful and fantastic appliance in the kitchen, it is essential to check the appliance's fundamental favorite tips and tricks.

1.Use little oil

When using an air fryer, use minimum oil since food placed in it does not need a lot of oil to crisp. Excess of the oil will drip out from food and stream to the bottom of the machine, thus producing smoke. Spay the food only with a fine oil mist.

Also, please do not add extra oils to deep-fried frozen food as they contain vast amounts of oils in breading. For example, Food substances like skin chicken thighs need no oil, but vegetables can require a little oil.

2.Preheating is unnecessary

It is not required to preheat the air fryer before cooking; doing so will alter the recipe's cooking time. Consider preheating if the recipe requires so.

3.Shake the air fryers basket

To achieve the best results, shake your food and turn it over at least once to get a crispy and lovely meal. Other air fryers have shake reminders that beep when the basket is fit for shaking. If your air fryer does not have one, you can set your reminder.

4.Utilize a spray-on oil by using a reusable bottle

Non-stick sprays such as pam can leave greasy residues on the air fryer basket, thus ruining non-stick coating. Therefore, they are not recommended. A refillable spray bottle is the best alternative and keeps the aerosol spray away from the air fryer.

5.Do not crowd the basket.

Even though you have a big air fryer with a large basket, as much food cannot fit the basket as you may think; food needs ample space and air circulation to ensure the food gets crispy. For instance, if you fill the basket with a whole bag of frozen fries, you won't achieve crispy food, unlike when you use half of the fries. Overcrowding the basket lengthens the cooking time in the air fryer.

6.Prevent sticking of food residue with parchment paper

This may not be necessary often, but when cooking delicate and sticky food substances, using parchment paper can help avoid sticking in the basket. For example, when cooking fish, you can use it to ensure sticky residue does not crumble.

7.Soak the basket immediately after it has cooled for an easy cleanup

Cleaning the basket after use efficiently needs prompt soaking. Soaking your air fryer components in hot soapy water eases the cleanup process by ensuring greasy ad sticky food residues will not dry on the surface of the pan or basket.

8.Cooking times are not the same.

Like any appliance, not all of them are designed the same with the same features. Also, cooking different recipes takes more or less time, depending on the kind of food. Ensure you keep an eye on getting your desired food cooked appropriately.

Strawberry & Nutella Pancakes

Prep time: 10 minutes

Cook time: 40 minutes

Serves 2-3

Pancakes have always been a British household breakfast ever since the 15th century. In more recent years, Nutella has become one of the more favourite ingredients for toppings, spreads, shakes, cakes etc. Our air fried pancakes are soft and spongy, with them being accompanied by Nutella provides a burst of chocolate goodness. Not to mention, the juicy strawberries give the pancakes that additional tangy/sweet finish.

Ingredients

- 240g wheat flour
- 40g melted butter
- 15g baking powder
- 200g halved strawberries
- ½ tsp kosher salt

- 240ml buttermilk
- 1 large egg
- 1 ½ tbsp Nutella per serving (optionally melted)
- ½ tsp vanilla extract
- 1cal butter fry spray (use as much as required)

Preparation Instructions

1. Using a stand mixer, whisk all the granulated Ingredients, which include: wheat flour, baking powder, and salt
2. Now take a medium sized bowl and beat an egg, followed by adding the buttermilk, vanilla extract, and melted butter
3. Amalgamate both dry and wet ingredients into one bowl, then stir thoroughly to form the pancake batter
4. Set the batter aside
5. Preheat the air fryer at 190°C for 4-5 minutes
6. Meanwhile, spray a 6" pizza pan generously, using the 1cal fry spray
7. Pour the pancake batter onto the pizza pan
8. Select the 'bake/roast' function on the air fryer at 200° for 3 minutes, if applicable to your machine
9. Retrieve the pancake and set aside
10. Repeat the whole process until all of the batter has been used
11. Divide the pancakes by 2 or 3 plates
12. Dollop and spread 1 ½ tbsp of Nutella on each serving of pancakes
13. Divide the strawberries by the amount of servings and place them on top of the Nutella

Avocado Loaded Egg Whites

Prep time: 5 minutes

Cook time: 10 minutes

Serves 4

A quick and easy air fryer breakfast. Boiled eggs are consumed globally, but removing the yolk and including some mashed avocado provides a unique creamy flavour and many vital nutrients.

Ingredients

- 8 medium eggs
- 120g mashed avocado
- 1 tsp sea salt
- 1 tsp ground black pepper

Preparation Instructions

1. Place the caged rack in the air fryer, if applicable
2. Pour in 400ml of water
3. Gently place the eggs on top of the rack
4. Select the 'pressure' setting at 'high', along with the appropriate lid, and a cook time of 7 minutes
5. Using kitchen tongs, remove the eggs from the air fryer and place them into ice water for a minute
6. Peel the eggs and place them back into the ice water
7. Slice the eggs in half and remove the egg yolks
8. Fill each halved egg white with ½ tbsp of avocado
9. Garnish the egg whites with sea salt and pepper

Cheese & Veg Omelette

Prep time: 5 minutes

Cook time: 10 minutes

Serves 4

The cheese & veg Omelette, or as the French like to call it 'omelette du fromage' is one of my all time favourite breakfasts. Our traditional variant offers a true explosion of flavours, from egg, 2 different cheeses, 3 colours of bell pepper, mushrooms and 2 different seasonings.

Ingredients

- 2 eggs
- 1 small onion
- ½ chopped red bell pepper
- 2 diced cherry tomatoes
- 2 diced mushrooms
- ½ chopped green bell pepper

- ½ chopped orange bell pepper
- 25g parmesan cheese
- ½ tsp ground black pepper
- 25g extra mature cheddar cheese
- 1/8 tsp Himalayan salt
- 1cal olive oil fry spray (use as needed)

Preparation Instructions

1. Preheat the air fryer at 180°C for 3-4 minutes
2. Crack and beat the eggs in a large bowl
3. Add all of the ingredients from the veg to the cheeses (except 1cal fry spray) and mix thoroughly
4. Pour the omelette mixture into a cake tin suitable for the air fryer
5. Select the 'bake/roast' setting at 180°C for 8-9 minutes, allowing the cheeses, egg and veg to amalgamate properly
6. Retrieve the omelette, cut it in half and place it into 2 plates to serve

Egg Burrito

Prep time: 15 minutes
Cook time: 6 minutes
Serves 4

Quite a simple and straight forward dish. The egg burrito has Mexican origins, but works fantastically on British taste buds. You can dine in with the burrito, or take it on the go.

Ingredients

- 4 eggs
- ½ tsp chili powder
- ⅛ tbsp ground black pepper
- 60g shredded Questo Fresco (orange Mexican cheese)
- 4 tbsp pre-prepared guacamole
- 1cal avocado fry spray (use as much as required)
- 60ml milk
- ¼ tsp sea salt
- 4 Twelve inch white tortillas
- 120g chopped avocado

Preparation Instructions

1. Preheat the air fryer at 180°C for 4-5 minutes
2. Beat the 4 eggs in a large mixing bowl
3. Toss in the milk, chilli, salt and pepper and stir thoroughly
4. Using a cake tin suitable for the air fryer, pour in the casserole/egg-basedIngredients
5. Select the 'bake/roast' air fryer feature at 180°C for 8-9 minutes
6. Using a wooden spoon, scramble the egg at the 4 minute mark of cooking
7. Meanwhile, layout the tortillas on a clean surface
8. Toss the cheese onto the tortillas
9. Retrieve the egg and divide it into 4 equal portions
10. Spread the egg onto the tortillas and wrap

11.Place the burritos into the air fryer to amalgamate the cheese for 3 minutes

12.Dollop a tbsp of guacamole at the top (optional) and serve

Simple Sweet Porridge

Prep time: 5 minutes

Cook time: 6 minutes

Serves 4

Oats is certainly a healthy British breakfast with a massive 5g of dietary fibre per serving. Our variant of air fried oats is very tasty with 4 additional sweet ingredients.

Ingredients

- 200g porridge oats
- 500ml milk or water
- 1 tbsp brown sugar
- 4 tbsp honey
- 160g raisins
- 300g blueberries

Preparation Instructions

1.Preheat the air fryer at 180°C for 3-4 minutes

2.Pour the oats, milk, raisins, and sugar into a mixing bowl and stir thoroughly

3.Pour the oats mixture into the air fryer barrel (closed bottom)

4.Set the air fryer to bake at 180°C for 10 minutes

5.Retrieve the oats and divide them into 4 bowls

6.Drizzle 1 tbsp honey and toss 75g of blueberries in each bowl before serving

Spicy Breakfast Potato's

Prep time: 3 minutes

Cook time: 13 minutes

Serves 2

This recipe is our spicy twist to the traditional British roast potato breakfast. If you can't tolerate spice, then simply refrain from adding the chilli flakes and paprika.

Ingredients

- 500g cube cut potatoes
- 1 tbsp flaxseed oil
- ½ tbsp chilli flakes
- ½ tbsp ground black pepper

- 1 tsp paprika
- 1 tsp garlic granules
- 2 tsp Worchester sauce

Preparation Instructions

1. Preheat the air fryer at 180°C for
2. Using a mixing bowl, combine all of the ingredients using your hands
3. If applicable, select the 'bake/roast' function on your air fryer at 200°C for 13 minutes
4. Toss the potatoes into the barrel of the air fryer
5. Retrieve the potatoes and divide them into 2 plates
6. Drizzle Worchester sauce on each portion of potatoes and serve

Sausage Breakfast

Prep time: 7 minutes
Cook time: 10 minutes
Serves 2

Ingredients

- 8 sausages (meat of choice)
- 1 tomato
- 1 white mushroom

Preparation Instructions

1. Preheat the air fryer at 180°C for 4-5 minutes
2. Chop the tomato in half from the middle
3. Chop the mushroom in half
4. Place the sausages in the air fryer at 200° for 10 minutes
5. At the 5 minute mark, place the tomatoes and mushrooms into the air fryer with the sausages
6. Retrieve and divide all of the ingredients into 2 dishes before serving

Toast Topped With Strawberry Jam

Prep time: 2 minutes
Cook time: 6 minutes
Serves 2
Strawberry Jam is a very traditional condiment to layer over crispy toast. It is quick and easy to prepare. In terms of flavour, toast and jam provides a combination of sweet and savoury.

Ingredients

- 4 tsp olive margarine

- 4 slices of bread (of choice)
- 4 tbsp strawberry Jam

Preparation Instructions

1. Using a tsp or butter knife, spread margarine on each slice of bread
2. Place the bread into the air fryer at 200°C for 6-7 minutes, to make crispy toast
3. Remove the toast from air fryer and put them into a plate (2 slices per plate)
4. Dollop and spread 1 tbsp of Jam on each slice of toast before serving

Berry & Syrup Waffles

Prep time: 12-15 minutes
Cook time: 40 minutes
Serves 2-3
The sweet waffle is very similar to the pancake, but perhaps different in texture. With our variant, we have gone with a very western type of waffle, incorporating toppings such as; maple syrup, berries, whipped cream and caster sugar.

Ingredients

- 240g wheat flour
- 40g melted butter
- 15g baking powder
- 100g blueberries
- Ready to use whipped cream
- ½ tsp vanilla extract
- 240ml buttermilk
- 1 large egg
- 100g raspberries
- 60ml maple syrup
- 20g caster sugar
- ½ tsp kosher salt

1cal butter fry spray (use as much as required)

Preparation Instructions

1. Using a stand mixer, whisk all the granulated Ingredients, which include: wheat flour, baking powder, and salt
2. Now take a medium sized bowl and beat an egg, followed by adding the buttermilk, vanilla extract, and melted butter
3. Amalgamate both dry and wet ingredients into one bowl, then stir thoroughly to form the waffle batter
4. Set the waffle batter aside
5. Preheat the air fryer at 190°C for 4-5 minutes
6. Meanwhile, spray a silicon waffle mould generously using 1cal butter fry spray. (As a side note, the silicon moulds will NOT melt with the cooking temperature)
7. Pour the waffle batter onto the waffle moulds
8. Select the 'bake/roast' function on the air fryer at 200° for 3 minutes, if applicable to your machine

9. Retrieve the waffles and set aside
10. Repeat the whole process until all of the batter has been used
11. Divide and pile up the waffles by 2 or 3 plates
12. Drizzle 2 tbsp of maple syrup on top of each serving of waffles
13. Divide the raspberries and blueberries by the amount of servings and place them on top
14. Spray a dollop of whipped cream on top of the berries
15. Dash the caster sugar on top of the waffles to finalise

Savoury Toast

Prep time: 10 minutes
Cook time: 15 minutes
Serves 4
Delicious toast with typical savoury British toppings, quite the contrast from the usual sweet Nutella and jams that many Brits enjoy.

Ingredients
For Toast
- 4 slices of bread
- 4 tsp of olive margarine

For eggs
- 8 medium eggs
- ¼ tsp sea salt
- ¼ tsp ground black pepper

For Chorizo
- 150g pre prepared sliced chorizo
- 40g finely diced coriander

For Other
- 1 Peeled avocado

Preparation Instructions
1. Place the caged rack in the air fryer
2. Pour in 400ml of water
3. Gently place the eggs on top of the rack
4. Select the 'pressure' setting at 'high' along with the appropriate lid (if applicable) and a Cook time of 7 minutes
5. Using kitchen tongs, remove the eggs from the air fryer and place them into ice water for a minute
6. Peel the eggs and place then back into the ice water
7. Apply ½ a tbsp on each slice of toast
8. Slice the eggs, sprinkle sea salt and pepper and set them aside

9. Slice the avocado
10. Apply 1 tsp of margarine to each slice of bread
11. Remove the water from the air fryer and insert the cooking barrel, if applicable
12. Place the bread and chorizo into the air fryer at 200° for 7 minutes
13. Retrieve the toast and chorizo
14. Place the toast on a plate, top with chorizo, coriander, avocado, sliced egg
15. Ensure that you have divided all of the food products equally across all 4 slices of toast

French Toast Sticks

Prep time: 5 minutes
Cook time: 10 minutes
Serves 4

French toast sticks, or as we call it in the UK 'eggy bread' was a Roman invention that dates back to the first century AD. French Toast is an amalgamation of egg, bread, milk, flour, and sugar, so it is sweet in taste, golden in appearance and crispy in texture, making it a great breakfast to start the day.

Ingredients

- 5 slices of oat bread
- 80ml milk
- 25g all-purpose flour
- ½ tsp vanilla extract

- 2 large eggs
- 40g white sugar
- 1 tsp ground cinnamon
- 1/8 tsp salt

Preparation Instructions

1. Preheat the air fryer at 180°C before making the French toast batter
2. Beat the eggs in a medium sized bowl
3. Add all of the ingredients into the bowl, except for the bread
4. Amalgamate all of the ingredients by stirring with a fork
5. Coat the bread by submerging it in the batter, but ensure you do not keep it in the batter for longer than a second too long, so that the bread does not dissolve and break apart
6. Place the coated bread in the air fryer and ramp up the temperature to 190°C for 5-6 minutes
7. Remove the French toast from the air fryer and slice vertically
8. Divide the French toast sticks by 4 and serve

Spinach & Fried Egg Pot

Prep time: 12-15 minutes
Cook time: 10 minutes
Serves 4

Ingredients

4 large egg
- 60ml milk
- 60g spinaches
- 30g thinly grated cheddar cheese
- 1 tsp ground black pepper
- 1cal olive oil fry spray

Preparation Instructions

1. Preheat the air fryer at 180°C for 4-5 minutes
2. Using the 1cal fry spray, grease the baking pots generously
3. Crack the eggs into the baking pots
4. Toss the 15g of spinach and pour 15ml of milk per baking pot, but ensure not to pop the egg yolk
5. Stir the ingredients around the egg white
6. Sprinkle cheese and season the eggs with pepper, equally across all 4 bake pots
7. Place the egg bake pots into the air fryer, at 180°C for 10 minutes, preferably on the 'air crisp' setting, if it is available for your air fryer
8. Retrieve the bake pots from the air fryer and serve

Banana & Peanut butter Bagel

Prep time: 2 minutes
Cook time: 6 minutes
Serves 2

The bagel is a German creation but has been adopted and adapted by many countries, like the UK and Eastern USA. Our recipe is traditional, as we opted for cinnamon and raisin bagels, filled with sweet and savoury fillings, also providing an amalgamation of crunchy and smooth.

Ingredients

- 2 cinnamon and raisin bagels
- 4 tsp olive margarine
- 2 tbsp crunchy peanut butter
- 2 large bananas

Preparation Instructions

1. Using a kitchen knife, cut the bagels horizontally to create 2 sliced halves
2. Spread 1 tsp of margarine on the inside of each sliced bagels
3. Place the bagels in the air fryer at 200°C for 6-7 minutes (crust layers facing down)
4. Meanwhile, peel and mash the bananas and set aside as 2 portions
5. Remove the bagels from the air fryer and put them on a plate (1 bagel per plate)
6. Inside each bagel, layer one side with 1 tbsp of peanut butter and the other side with mashed

banana

7.Sandwich the bagel together and serve

Chocolate Protein Pancake

Prep time: 5 minutes

Cook time: 18 minutes

Serves 2

In the last decade or so, the fitness culture has risen substantially in the UK. For this reason, we have put together an air fryer recipe for 'gym goers' and 'fitness freaks'. This recipe makes a tasty chocolate chip protein pancake that yields over 40g of protein per serving.

Ingredients

- 3 scoops of whey protein powder (90g)
- 120g dark chocolate chip cookie dough mix
- 100ml milk
- 2 eggs
- 1cal olive oil fry spray
- 2 tbsp Nutella

Preparation Instructions

1.Preheat the air fryer at 180°C for 4-5 minutes

2.Toss all of the ingredients into a stand mixer and whisk together (Except fry spray)

3.Using the 1cal fry spray, spray a 6" pizza pan

4.Pour the protein pancake mixture into the pizza pan

5.Place the pizza pan in the air fryer to cook for 2-3 minutes

6.Repeat the process until all of the mixture is used. The mixture should yield around 6 pancakes

7.Divide the total number of pancakes into 2 plates

8.Dollop and spread 1 tbsp of Nutella on top of each serving (melting Nutella is optional)

Scramble Egg Whites

Prep time: 12-15 minutes

Cook time: 8-10 minutes

Serves 4

This is the much 'healthier' variant of the scrambled egg. This variant is much lower in fat and yields around 14g of protein per serving.

Ingredients

- 12 large egg

- 60ml semi-skimmed milk
- 100g spinaches
- 30g finely chopped coriander
- 1 tsp ground black pepper
- 1 tsp sea salt
- 1cal olive oil fry spray

Preparation Instructions

1. Preheat the air fryer at 180°C for 4-5 minutes
2. Using the 1cal frying spray, grease a 10" pizza pan generously
3. Crack all 12 eggs into a large bowl
4. Using a tbsp, scoop out the egg yolks and dispose
5. Add the salt, pepper, semi-skimmed milk and spinach
6. Stir to combine the ingredients
7. Pour the egg whites into the pizza pan and place it in the air fryer at 180°C for 8-10 minutes
8. Continue to check the egg whites every 2 minutes and scramble
9. Retrieve the egg whites from the air fryer and garnish with coriander
10. Divide the scrambled egg whites by 4 and plate them up

Marmalade Bacon

Prep time: 6 minutes
Cook time: 8 minutes
Serves 2

Bacon is a staple food source amongst British people. Marmalade is a sweet/sour orange jam that was adopted by Britain. Marmalade was made popular by the British icon/fictional character Paddington bear, who was founded in 1958. Layering marmalade over bacon gives it that sweet, sour, and savoury combination, for a tasty breakfast addition.

Ingredients

- 12 bacon Strips (meat of your choice)
- 45g marmalade

Preparation Instructions

1. Preheat the air fryer to 180°C for 4-5 minutes
2. Place the bacon strips into the air fryer for 5 minutes at 180°C
3. Flip the bacon strips and leave them in the air fryer for another 3 minutes
4. Retrieve the bacon and brush over them with traditional British marmalade and serve

English Sheppard's Pie

Prep time: 20 minutes

Cook time: 50 minutes

Serves 6-10

The Sheppard's pie originated in Northern England. Our variant is loyal to the great British ingredients and methodology of preparation, hence why we have referred to it as the 'British Sheppard's Pie'. The Sheppard's pie contains a variety of ingredients including meats, vegetables and broths, thereby it has been widely accepted as a delicious and nutritious main recipe all around the UK.

Ingredients

- 500g British mince lamb
- 30g parmesan cheese
- 120ml lamb broth
- 25g cooking flour
- 15g chopped rosemary
- ¼ tbsp Himalayan salt
- 2 minced garlic cloves
- 100g diced fennel
- 1 tbsp Worcestershire sauce
- 2 tbsp fine chopped parsley
- 240g British mature cheddar
- 900g hash brown
- 30g Butter
- 500g chopped mushrooms
- 30g tomato puree
- ½ tbsp ground pepper
- 100g diced onion
- 60g diced carrot
- 1 tbsp British mustard

Preparation Instructions

1. First, we are required to add Butter to the barrel of your air fryer, preferably using the 'instant pot duo crisp'.
2. Select the Sear or Sauté function employing 'high' heat.
3. Add and stir the mushrooms, followed by 1/8 tbsp of salt and ¼ tbsp of the ground pepper
4. After the 4-5 minute mark, the mushrooms should begin to appear brown in colour, where you will then need to add and stir the onions, fennel, carrot, and rosemary for 4-5 minutes
5. Add the remainder of salt and pepper
6. At this point, we need to add and stir the beef mince and cook it until it becomes brown and crumbly in texture (4-5 minutes)
7. Dollop the tomato puree into the air fryer barrel and stir for 50-60 seconds
8. Transition to the 'keep warm' if applicable for your specific air fryer, or temporarily turn off the air fryer completely
9. In preparation for the 'pressure' cooking function, employ all the appropriate attachments for your air fryer

10. Dollop the lamb broth, mustard and Worcester sauce
11. Stir these ingredients thoroughly and then select the 'pressure' function on the 'High' setting
12. Release the pressure after a duration of 5 minutes
13. Revert back to the 'sear/sauté' function at a 'high' temperature
14. Meanwhile, using a stand mixer, whisk the flour with 30-50ml of water
15. Add and stir flour-based mixture with the lamb
16. Continue cooking for 3 minutes to form a thick texture
17. Distribute the hash brown and cheddar on the top of the meat-based mixture
18. Select the air fryer 'bake/roast' function at 205°C for 30-35 minutes or until the cheese displays a golden/brown appearance
19. To finalise the Sheppard's pie, sprinkle with parmesan cheese
20. Remove the barrel from the air fryer and cut 6 large squares or 10 small ones to serve

Lasagne

Prep time: 75 minutes
Cook time: 75 minutes
Serves 6

Lasagne has Greek origins, but has been widely adopted as a 'main' in British culinary. Lasagne was first introduced during the first quarter of the 19th century in the Victorian era. It is saucy, soft in texture, and very tasty, thus earning its place as a 'winner for dinner' in our books.

Ingredients

- 500g good quality lean minced lamb
- tsp dried oregano or dried mixed herbs
- 400ml vegetable broth
- 1 large egg
- 200g grated British mature cheddar
- ¾ nutmeg

- 2 crushed garlic cloves
- 500g sliced mushrooms
- 50g tomato ketchup
- 300ml double cream
- 9 sheets of fresh lasagne

Preparation Instructions

1. Preheat the air fryer for 4-5 minutes at 180°C
2. Select the 'air crisp' function at 180°C for 6 minutes and add and stir 250g of the beef mince, using a wooden spoon every 2 minutes
3. Retrieve the cooked mince and place it in a bowl
4. Toss the other half of the mince (250g) into the air fryer, but add garlic and oregano
5. Allow the mince to cook for 6 minutes, then mix in the previously browned portion of mince
6. Add the mushrooms, veg broth, ketchup, and the remainder salt/pepper
7. Stir well to amalgamate all of the ingredients
8. Allow the ingredients to cook for another 30 minutes, then switch to a 'keep warm' function if applicable to your air fryer

9. Stir the ingredients every 10 minutes
10. Meanwhile, beat the egg in a large bowl using a fork
11. Using a stand mixer on a slow setting, combine double cream and 100g of cheese with the egg making a cheese sauce
12. Layer a dish with lasagne and add boiling to pre-cook for 5 minutes
13. Employ a baking pot suitable for your air fryer and spread 2 heaped wooden spoons of the meat mix on top
14. Using kitchen tongs, layer 3 sheets of lasagne onto this meat mix
15. Drizzle 4 tbsp of the cheese on top of the lasagne sheets
16 Dollop spread half of the remaining meat mix
17 Apply another layer of lasagne (3 sheets)
18. Once again, dollop and spread the remaining meat mix, followed by the last 3 sheets of lasagne
19. Pour the rest of the cheese sauce evenly over the last layer of lasagne
20. To finalise, sprinkle the remaining 100g of cheddar and nutmeg over the top of the bake
21. Select the 'bake/roast' setting at 180°C for 25-30 minutes and gently place the lasagne bake pot inside
22. Open the air fryer and leave the lasagne to cool for 5 minutes
23. Retrieve the lasagne and cut it inton6 equal squares to serve

'Bangers' & Mash

Prep time: 30 minutes
Cook time: 90 minutes
Serves 7
In 2009, Bangers and mash were rated Britain's comfort food in a survey by 'Good Food'. The meal consists of a big dish of creamy mash covered with saucy sausages and crispy onions.

Ingredients
For Sausages
- 10 sausages (meat of choice)
- 200g finely sliced onion
- 1 bay leaf
- 1 tsp soy sauce
- 50g finely diced coriander
- 20g butter
- 1 thyme sprig
- 1 tbsp Worchester sauce
- 400ml beef stock

For Mash
- 10 large white potatoes
- 50ml milk
- 1/8 tsp ground pepper
- 200ml double cream
- 1/8 tsp Himalayan salt

Preparation Instructions
1. Preheat the air fryer to 180°C for 3-4 minutes

2. Create 3 small incisions on the centre of each potato with a knife. This prevents the potatoes from bursting whilst cooking

3. Using the air fryer 'bake/roast' setting, cook the potatoes for 1hr at 180°C

4. Retrieve the potatoes from the air fryer and split in half using a knife

5. Extract the potato with a tbsp and toss it into a bowl

6. Mash the potatoes and dash salt and pepper

7. In order to make a creamy mash, add the double cream and milk, then stir thoroughly

8. Set the mash aside in a large dish and cover with foil

9. Place the sausages in the air fryer at 180° for 10 minutes, or the 'sear/sauté' function on a medium heat

10. Retrieve the sausages and set aside

11. Reset the air fryer and toss in the onions, butter, sprig, bay leaf for 10 minutes

12. Put the sausages back into the air fryer with other ingredients and pour in the Worchester, soy and beef stock

13. All these food products should be baked for 20 minutes

14. Remove the ingredients, dollop and spread them on top of the mash

15. Dash the coriander on top of the bangers and mash

Chicken Casserole

Prep time: 30 minutes
Cook time: 30 minutes
Serves 4
For this specific recipe, you must have the Ninja Foodi 8-in-1, or at least something similar. The chicken casserole has a concoction of flavours and is best served with mash or rice

Ingredients

- 5 Boneless/Skinless chicken thighs
- 2 cloves of crushed garlic
- 2 tsp dehydrated mixed herbs
- 550g chopped carrots
- 175g frozen green beans
- 700ml chicken stock

- 45g chopped onion
- 1 tbsp flaxseed oil
- 2 Bay leaves
- 2 chopped celery stalks
- 175g broccoli
- 2 ¼ chicken gravy granules

Preparation Instructions

1. Select the 'sear/sauté' function on the ninja foodi for 6 minutes

2. Pour in the flaxseed oil, followed by the onions

3. Once the onions have softened, toss in the chicken thighs

4. After the 6 minute cooking duration, turn the air fryer off and add the remainder of the ingredients, with the exception of the green veg

5. Change the ninja foodi applications for pressure set for 20 minutes

6. Revert back to the 'sear/sauté' function and toss in the green vegetables
7. All the ingredients to sear for 4 minutes
8. Add some gravy granules
9. Simmer the food content for another 3-4 minutes
10. Retrieve the casserole and serve

Full Size Fish & Leak Pie

Prep time: 20 minutes

Cook time: 105 minutes

Serves 6-8

The Fish & Leak Pie! a truly British dish that originated in Scotland around the 16th century. Fish pies were generally eaten as a delicious Friday evening dinner across millions of families across Great Britain. The fish and Leak pie is very creamy, soft and full of fish flavour

Ingredients

For Fish

- 125g skinless smoked haddock chunks
- 10 fresh king prawns
- 25g dijon mustard
- ¼ tsp ground nutmeg
- 200ml double cream
- 20ml lemon juice

- 125g skinless salmon chunks
- 100g butter
- 3 thin sliced leeks
- 100ml dry vermouth
- 30g chopped chives
- 3-4g lemon zest

For Mash

- 7 large white potatoes
- 60g grated extra mature cheddar
- 60g grated parmesan cheese
- 200ml double cream
- 50ml milk
- 1/8 tsp Himalayan salt
- 1/8 tsp ground pepper

Preparation Instructions

1. Start by making 3 small incisions on the centre of each potatoes with a knife, this prevents the potatoes from bursting whilst cooking
2. Using the Air fryer 'bake/roast' setting, cook the potatoes for 1hr at 180°C
3. Meanwhile, employ a large frying pan and apply butter
4. Place the leeks on the melted butter and cook for 10 minutes on low-medium heat
5. Drizzle the nutmeg, mustard, vermouth, and cream onto the leeks
6. Simmer these ingredients for 10 minutes
7. Turn off the heat to the lowest setting and add chives, lemon zest and lemon juice

8. Gently place the fish ingredients onto to the creamy leeks and stir
9. Dollop the ingredients into a medium bake pot
10. Retrieve the potatoes from the air fryer and split in half using a knife
11. Extract the potato with a tbsp and toss it into a bowl
12. Mash the potatoes and dash of salt and pepper
13. In order to make creamy mash, add the double cream and milk then stir thoroughly
14. Dollop the mash on top of the fish ingredients
15. Finalise the bake by dashing the cheeses on top
16. Once again, select the 'bake/roast' function at 180°C on the air fryer for 30 minutes
17. Retrieve the leek and fish pie and cut into 6-8 slices and serve

Rump & Sweet Potato Chips

Prep time: 10 minutes
Cook time: 20-25 minutes
Serves 3
Steak and chips is a very British main. Our air fryer variant has used Rump and sweet potato, which are tasty and nutritious food products.

Ingredients
Steak
- Rump steak 3x200g
- 1 tbsp olive oil
- ¼ tsp Himalayan salt
- ¼ tsp ground black pepper
- 1 tbsp unsalted butter
- 1 crushed garlic clove
- 1 ¼ tbsp rosemary

Chips
- 3 large sweet potatoes
- ¼ tsp Himalayan salt

Preparation Instructions
1. Combine the ingredients by rubbing them into the meat and allow 2-3hrs allows for the flavours to infuse
2. Preheat the air fryer at 180°C for 4-5 minutes
3. Place the meats inside and for 10-15 minutes
4. Meanwhile, peel and cut the sweet potatoes into thick chips
5. Season the chips with a Himalayan salt
6. Retrieve the steaks and set on a cooking board to cool
7. Place the sweet potato chips into the air fryer for 10-12 minutes

8.Divide the sweet potato chips into 2 portions and plate them up, along with the rump steak

Lincolnshire Haslet

Prep time: 10 minutes
Cook time: 105 minutes
Serves 8
Haslet was originally a European dish that made its way around the UK and USA through colonialism. Haslet is traditionally made from pork meat, but can be made from different meats.

Ingredients

- 1000g finely chopped pork belly
- 250g finely chopped onion
- 2 large beaten egg
- 50g day old dry bread crumbs
- 2 tbsp chopped sage
- 2 tsp sea salt
- 2 tsp ground black pepper
- 3 tbsp olive oil

Preparation Instructions

1. Start by preheating the air fryer at 200°C for 4-5 minutes
2. Toss the pork meat into a large bowl
3. Add the onions, bread crumbs, egg, thyme, salt and pepper
4. Hand mix and amalgamate the ingredients
5. Dollop this pork mixture into a large loaf pan (if suitable for your air fryer), or 2 small loaf pans
6. Brush the pork over with oil
7. Cover the load pan with foil and place in the air fryer at 180°C for 60 minutes
8. Remove the foil and cook for another 45 minutes
9. Retrieve the haslet and set it aside to cool
10. Slice the haslet into 8 portions and serve

Turkey Sausages and Potato Dish

Prep time: 15 minutes
Cook time: 20 minutes
Serves 6

Ingredients

- 1.2kg potatoes

- 530g/8 Turkey sausages
- 1¼ onion
- 45ml olive oil
- 1¼ tbsp all-purpose seasoning
- ¾ tbsp garlic granules
- ¼ tsp sea salt
- ¼ tsp ground black pepper

Preparation Instructions

1. Preheat the air fryer at 200°C for 8 minutes
2. Meanwhile, peel and dice the potatoes into small cubes
3. Wash the potatoes under cold running water, using a sieve
4. Toss the potatoes into a large bowl
5. Hand mix with the 4 seasonings (garlic, salt, pepper, all-purpose) and 1 tbsp of olive oil
6. Now toss the potatoes in the air fryer at 180°C for 12 minutes
7. Meanwhile, chop the British sausages into chunks and place them in a medium bowl
8. Drizzle the remainder of the oil on to the sausages
9. Chop up the onion into cubes and add them on top of the Sausages
10. Amalgamate these 2 food products with the potatoes
11. Air fry the sausage and potatoes for another 8-10 minutes
12. Retrieve the sausage and potatoes and them into a large dish
13. Put the dish on the dinner table to serve

Beef Haslet (meatloaf)

Prep time: 10 minutes
Cook time: 20 minutes
Serves 4-5
As you may know, haslet is traditionally made from pork, but beef works just as well and, in my opinion, is more taste bud friendly. The meat crumbles in the mouth and is saturated with different flavours and textures.

Ingredients

- 500g beef mince (80% beef)
- 1 large beaten egg
- 1 tbsp chopped thyme
- 1 tsp ground black pepper
- 1 ½ tbsp flaxseed oil
- 125g finely chopped onion
- 25g bread crumbs
- 1 tsp sea salt
- 2 mushrooms sliced into wedges

Preparation Instructions

1. Start by preheating the air fryer at 200°C for 4-5 minutes

2.Toss the minced beef into a large bowl

3.Add the onions, bread crumbs, egg, thyme, salt and pepper

4.Hand mix and amalgamate the ingredients

5.Dollop this meat mixture into a loaf pan to create a slab of meat

6.Peirce mushrooms into the slab of meat and brush them over with oil

7.Place the meat slab in the air fryer at 180°C for 25-30 minutes

8.Retrieve the beef haslet and set it aside to cool

9.Slice the beef haslet into 4-5 portions and serve

Classic Fish & Chips

Prep time: 15 minutes

Cook time: 30 minutes

Serves 4

Fried fish and chips are commonly associated with British culinary cuisine. This was largely due to the scarcity of food in the country during WW2, where people were forced to improvise with the ingredients that were available, HEY PRESTO! Out came fish and chips. When done properly, The fish should be soft and flaky, whilst the outer shell is crispy. The fish is served with thick cut potato pieces, which we refer to as 'chips'.

Ingredients

For Fish

- 4 cod fillets (250g each)
- 80g dried breadcrumbs
- ¼ tsp ground pepper
- 45g all purpose flour
- Dollop of tomato ketchup (optional)

- 1 Large egg
- 20g grated parmesan cheese
- ¼ tsp sea salt
- 30ml water

For Chips

- 2 Large potatoes
- 2 tbsp peanut oil
- ¼ tbsp sea salt
- ¼ tbsp ground pepper
- Vinegar

Preparation Instructions

1.Preheat the air fryer at 200°C for 6 minutes

2.Peel and cut the potatoes into thick chips

3.Using a large bowl combine all of the 'For Chips' ingredients

4.Hand toss and fold the chips, ensuring that the potato is covered in the spices

5.Place the chips into the air fryer and select the 'air crisp' or 'air fry' function for 10-20 minutes

6.Retrieve the chips once they become golden brown in colour and crispy on the outside

7. Whilst the chips are air frying, we employ 3 more bowls
8. In one of the bowls, combine the flour and pepper with a fork
9. In the second bowl, beat an egg with additional water
10. In the third bowl, mix the breadcrumbs and Parmesan
11. Treacle sea salt onto the cod fillets
12. Coat the cod fillets with the flour mixture, then dip them into the egg mixture, followed by the breadcrumb mixture
13. Ensure that the cod fillets are fully covered with breadcrumbs
14. Retrieve the air fried chips and toss them into an isolated warmer container or a plate, which you will cover with foil
15. Turn the air fryer back on, selecting the 'air crisp' function for 10-15 minutes
16. Once the cod becomes golden brown in appearance, remove them from the air fryer and plate them up
17. Sprinkle vinegar on top of the chips (optional), then divide the chips by 4 and place them next to the fish
18. Add a dollop of tomato ketchup on the plate as a condiment

Chill Con Carne

Prep time: 15 minutes
Cook time: 45 minutes
Serves 4-5
Chilli con carni was originally a Mexican dish, but accepted by the people of Britain, who can tolerate spices. Chilli con carni is generally very caloric dense with beef mince, kidney beans and a variety of herbs & spices.

Ingredients

- 500g beef mince (80% lean)
- 50g chopped tomatoes
- 30g tomato purée
- 1/8 tsp ground black pepper
- 1 tsp ground coriander
- 500g kidney beans
- 1 finely diced red pepper
- 125g thinly sliced onion
- 350ml beef stock
- 1/8 tsp sea salt
- 1 ½ tsp hot chilli powder
- 1 tbsp flaxseed oil
- 1 finely diced red chilli

Preparation Instructions

1. Preheat the air fryer to 180°C for 4-5 minutes
2. Pour the oil into the barrel of the air fryer
3. Toss the onions, peppers and chillies in, then leave the ingredients to cook for 5 minutes
4. Add the beef mince into the air fryer for 5 minutes, and break it up after 2 minutes of the cooking duration

5. Now, create a stock mixture by whisking the ground spices, tomato puree, and 2/3 of the beef stock in a medium sized bowl
6. Pour this mixture into the air fryer to combine it with the minced beef
7. Cook the food content for another 25 minutes
8. Stir the content every 8 minutes for short intervals
9. Combine the remainder of the beef stock with the canned beans, then add them to the mix
10. Cook the contents for another 10 minutes
11. Retrieve and stir the chilli con carni, then serve

Avacado Salad With Spicy Chorizo

Prep time 3 minutes
Cook time: 20 minutes
Serves 4

The recipe puts together a 'healthy' and colourful meal with a variety of salad and salty/spicy chorizo. This meal certainly classifies as a main course, as it has a reasonable amount of calories from the avocado and chorizo, perfect for those observing a low carbohydrate diet.

Ingredients

- 160g Spicy Chorizo
- 200g baby leaf/herb salad
- 1 ½ sliced Avocado
- 30ml apple cider vinegar (ACV)
- 1 shredded ciabatta
- 1/8 tsp brown sugar
- 300g diced tomatoes
- 60ml olive oil

Preparation Instructions

1. Pour half of the olive oil into the barrel of the air fryer and apply the 'sear/sauté' function, if applicable (or 180°C)
2. Toss in the ciabatta and cook for 9-10 minutes to make them crispy
3. Retrieve the ciabatta with kitchen tongs and start collating the salad bowls
4. Place the chorizo in the air fryer for 2-3 minutes, dehydrating the meat
5. Toss the tomatoes on top of the chorizo, to cook for another 2-3 minutes
6. Pour in the ACV and sugar to season the food content whilst it is cooking
7. Finalise the ingredients, by adding the remainder of the oil, avacado, salad
8. Retrieve all of the food content in the air fryer, including the by product juices
9. Place on top of the salad bowls to serve

Chicken Tikka Masala With Naan

Prep time: 5 minutes

Cook time: 15 minutes

Serves 4

Perhaps to your surprise, the chicken tikka masala is as British as food can get. Although the dish has south Asian influences, it was derived in the northern UK, Glasgow in Scotland to be precise, around the 70s. It was actually created to cater for the native English, who at the time had taste buds suited for milder spice.

Ingredients

For chicken/marinade
- 750g chicken breast chunks
- 20g tandoori masala
- 20g bio yogurt
- 20g all-purpose flour
- ½ tbsp Garam masala
- ¼ tbsp cumin powder
- ½ tbsp paprika
- ½ tbsp garlic paste
- 1 tbsp olive oil
- 1cal olive oil fry spray
- ¼ - ½ tbsp Himalayan salt

For tikka masala sauce
- 125g diced onion
- 250ml water
- 60g tomato puree
- 20g paprika
- 20g butter
- 25g honey
- 60ml double cream
- 450ml tomato sauce
- ½ tbsp garlic paste
- ¼ tbsp cumin powder

Other
- 4 naans or Garlic naans
- 20g diced coriander

Preparation Instructions

1. Place the chicken cubes in a bowl and simply dollop all of the 'for chicken/marinade' ingredients

2. Hand mix and rub the masalas into the chicken breast cubes
3. Set the chicken aside for 40 minutes
4. Place the barrel/instant pot into the air fryer and preheat it at 180°C for 5-6 minutes
5. Toss the diced onions into the air fryer and cover thoroughly with 1cal fry spray
6. Spread the chicken breast around the barrel of the air fryer
7. Pour oil on top of the chicken breast
8. Set the air fryer to 180°C for 8-10 minutes
9. Using oven gloves retrieve the chicken tikka and set it aside to separate from the onions
10. Now for the tikka masala, select the 'sear/saute' at medium and toss in butter (if applicable, or 180°C)
11. Add the crispy onions back into the air fryer for 40 seconds
12. Pour in the tomato sauce, ginger, and garlic for 1 ½ minutes
13. Dash in the 'for tikka masala' spices, including; garam masala, cumin, and paprika, then top with honey
14. Pour in the water to prevent the ingredients from burning
15. Now pressure cook the foot content on a high setting for 2 minutes
16. Add the double cream, chicken tikka and stir
17. Set the curry aside to cool
18. Meanwhile, place the naans in the air fryer to heat up for 2 minutes
19. Retrieve the naan to consume them with the chicken tikka masala

Turkey Mince Pasta Bake

Prep time: 5 minutes
Cook time: 20 minutes
Serves 2-3
Pasta bakes are a very Italian dish and sometimes with a British twist. They make the perfect main for dinner, with the main ingredients being pasta, cheese and mince.

Ingredients
- 250g turkey minced meat
- 125g diced onions
- 1 tbsp flaxseed oil
- 1 diced yellow bell pepper
- 1/8 tsp sea salt
- 1/8 tsp ground black pepper
- 450g plain boiled pasta
- 250ml pasta sauce
- 60g grated cheddar cheese

Preparation Instructions

1. Depending on your air fryer, select the 'sear/saute' function at medium heat or use a stove and pan
2. Start by pouring oil into the barrel of the air fryer for 3-4 minutes
3. Incorporate the onions and bell pepper for 3-4 minutes
4. Toss in the minced turkey to brown, and treacle with salt/pepper
5. Dollop the pasta sauce and stir thoroughly
6. Transfer the food content into a baking dish and sprinkle the cheddar on top
7. Now set the air fryer to 180°C
8. Place the baking dish in the air fryer and cook for 10-12 minutes
9. Retrieve the pasta bake and serve

Roast Duck On Creamy Mash

Prep time: 5 minutes
Cook time: 20 minutes
Serves 2
Roast Duck is delicate food source, best served on a bed of creamy mash, rice or plum sauce.

Ingredients
- 2 large skinless duck breasts
- 1 thyme sprig
- 1 star anise
- 30g butter

For Mash
- 5 large white potatoes
- 100ml double cream
- 50ml milk
- 1/8 tsp Himalayan salt
- 1/8 tsp ground pepper

Preparation Instructions
1. Preheat the air fryer at 180°C for 5-6 minutes
2. Sprinkle salt and pepper on top of the duck breasts
3. Place the duck breast in the air fryer for 6-7 minutes
4. Flip the duck breasts and dollop butter, thyme, and star anise on top
5. Allow the duck to cook for another 10-15 minutes
6. Retrieve the duck and juices, then wrap them in foil to set aside
7. Create 3 small incisions on the centre of each potato with a knife. This prevents the potatoes from bursting whilst cooking
8. Using the air fryer 'bake/roast' setting, cook the potatoes for 1hr at 180°C
9. Retrieve the potatoes from the air fryer and split in half using a knife

10. Extract the potato with a tbsp and toss it into a bowl
11. Mash the potatoes and dash salt and pepper
12. In order to make a creamy mash, add the double cream and milk, then stir thoroughly
13. Equally divide the creamy mash on 4 plates
14. Cut each duck breast in half
15. Place each half with the duck juices on top of each portion of mash, then serve

Classic Jacket Potato (Beans & Cheese)

Prep time: 5 minutes
Cook time: 50 minutes
Serves 4
You've got to love a good ol' British jacket potato. Hot jacket potatoes have been trending in British culinary since the 19th century, where they were commonly sold as street food during the cold autumn and winter months. Jacket potatoes have a soft base with a crispy skin. I must say, baked beans and cheese make the best fillings, which is also very nostalgic school dinners.

Ingredients
- 4 large potatoes
- 60g butter (4 tbsp)
- 1 tsp ground black pepper (optional)
- 1 tsp chilli flakes (optional)
- 500g baked beans
- 180g cheddar cheese

Preparation Instruction
1. Preheat the air fryer at 180° for 5 minutes
2. Make multiple insertions in the potato with a fork, ensuring they do not burst whilst baking
3. Place the potatoes into the air fryer and select the 'bake/roast' function at 200° for 50 minutes (if applicable)
4. Meanwhile, place the baked beans in the microwave or cooking pan for 2 minutes
5. Retrieve the potatoes and cut down the centre of the potatoes
6. Plate the potatoes up and layer a tbsp of butter in the centres
7. Divide the baked beans by 4 and dollop them in the centre of each potato
8. Top the hot baked beans with cheese, which should melt it partially
9. Season the potatoes with ground black pepper, chilli flakes (optional) and then serve

Simple Salmon and Asparagus

Prep time: 6 minutes

Cook time: 10-12 minutes

Serves 5

Salmon is a nutritious fish packed with protein and omega 3 fish oils. Salmon can be very quick and easy to cook, which can serve as a great main course for dinner

Ingredients

- 5 Salmon fillets
- 1 ¼ tsp sea salt
- 1 ¼ tsp ground pepper
- ½ tbsp flaxseed oil
- 4 stalks of asparagus

Preparation Instructions

1. Pre-heat the air fryer at 180°C for 5 minutes
2. Using a fork and small bowl to mix all of the ingredients, except the salmon and asparagus
3. Rub this spice type paste into the salmon
4. Select the 'grill' function on the air fryer if applicable
5. Place the salmon and the 4 stalks of asparagus into the barrel of the air fryer for 10-12 minutes

Spicy King Prawns

Prep time: 6 minutes

Cook time: 8-10 minutes

Serves 4

Spicy King Prawn is a very oriental dish. As you may know, the UK is very multi-cultural and diverse, therefore many of the British Public should be aware of the Spicy King Prawns. The Spicy King Prawns provide an explosion of sweet and spicy flavours, which can be eaten as an appetiser or main course if co-ingested with stir fry vegetables and carbohydrate-rich food source like wok style rice or noodles.

Ingredients

- 30 Fresh King Prawns
- 1 tbsp chilli powder
- 1 tbsp ground pepper

- 30ml sweet chilli sauce
- 45ml sesame seed oil
- 2 minced garlic cloves
- ¾ tbsp Chinese salt

Preparation Instructions

1. Preheat the air fryer at 180°C for 4-5 minutes
2. Wash the King Prawns thoroughly
3. Toss them into a large bowl, amalgamate all of the ingredients by hand mixing them
4. Place the King Prawns in the air fryer and select the 'air crisp' setting for 8-10 minutes
5. Remove the King Prawns and plate them up

Fish & Leek Pie Pots

Prep time: 20 minutes

Cook time: 90-105 minutes

Serves 6

The Fish & Leak Pie! a truly British dish that originated in Scotland around the 16th century. The leak and fish pie is normally eaten as a big wholesome family pie, but our variant has used individual bake pots than can be eaten with friends and stored in the refrigerator for later. The fish and Leak pie is very creamy, soft and full of fish flavour

Ingredients

For Fish

- 125g skinless smoked haddock chunks
- 10 fresh king prawns
- 25g dijon mustard
- ¼ tsp ground nutmeg
- 200ml double cream
- 20ml lemon juice

- 125g skinless salmon chunks
- 100g butter
- 3 thin sliced leeks
- 100ml dry vermouth
- 30g chopped chives
- 3-4g lemon zest

For Mash

- 7 large white potatoes
- 60g grated extra mature cheddar
- 60g grated parmesan cheese
- 200ml double cream
- 50ml milk
- 1/8 tsp Himalayan salt
- 1/8 tsp ground pepper

Preparation Instructions

1. Start by making 3 small incisions on the centre of each potatoes with a knife, this prevents the

potatoes from bursting whilst cooking

2.Using the Air fryer 'bake/roast' setting, cook the potatoes for 1hr at 180°C

3.Meanwhile, employ a large frying pan and apply butter

4.Place the leeks on the melted butter and cook for 10 minutes on low-medium heat

5.Drizzle the nutmeg, mustard, vermouth, and cream onto the leeks

6.Simmer these ingredients for 10 minutes

7.Turn off the heat to the lowest setting and add chives, lemon zest and lemon juice

8.Gently place the fish ingredients onto to the creamy leeks and stir

9.Divide these ingredients into 4 and add them into single bake pots

10.Retrieve the potatoes from the air fryer and split in half using a knife

11.Extract the potato with a tbsp and toss it into a bowl

12.Mash the potatoes and dash of salt and pepper

13.In order to make creamy mash, add the double cream and milk then stir thoroughly

14.Divide this creamy mash into 4 and dollop on top of the bake pots

15.Top the pots with the 2 cheeses and place them into the barrel of the air fryer

16.Once again, select the 'bake/roast' function on the air fryer for 20 minutes until golden in colour

17.Retrieve the bake pots and serve

Fish fingers & Mushy peas

Prep time: 10 minutes

Cook time: 15 minutes

Serves 2-3

Fish fingers & mush peas is another classic British dish, perfectly served as a dinner for kids after school or as an appetiser for adults.

Ingredients

- 500g of vertically slices haddock (10-12 Fingers)
- Cut in half horizontally if you want smaller bite size fingers (20-24)
- 65g all-purpose flour
- 1 tsp sea salt
- 1 tsp ground pepper
- ½ tsp paprika
- 2 large eggs
- 50g of crushed plain cornflakes or dried bread crumbs
- 250g of mushy peas
- 1 Dollop of ketchup

Preparation Instructions

1.Preheat the air fryer at 180°C for 5 minutes

2. Meanwhile, season the haddock with ½ tsp of the sea salt and set aside for 45 minutes to remove the moisture from the fish
3. Using a bowl and fork, add and combine the remainder salt, pepper, paprika and flour
4. In a separate bowl, add the dried bread crumbs
5. Beat the egg in to another bowl
6. Dunk the haddock fingers into the flour mixture, followed by egg and then the breadcrumbs
7. Select the 'air crisp' function at 200°C for 10 minutes
8. Microwave the mushy peas for 1 minute or 3 minutes with the fish fingers at the 12 minute mark (optional)
9. Divide the mushy peas by 2 or 3 and plate them up
10. Flip the fish fingers after 10 minutes and cook for another 5 minutes
11. Retrieve the fish fingers, divide and plate them up
12. Dollop some tomato ketchup onto the plates as a condiment (optional)

Air Fried Whitebait with Lime

Prep time: 5 minutes
Cook time: 10 minutes
Serves 4
A very simple dish that can serve as a quick snack or appetiser.

Ingredients

- 500g Anchovies
- 125g all-purpose flour
- 1 tbsp sea salt
- 45ml olive oil
- 1 lime chopped into wedges

Preparation Instructions

1. Preheat the air fryer at 180°C for 4-5 minutes
2. Using a small bowl, mix the flour and sea salt
3. Place the anchovies in another bowl, then add and hand mix olive oil
4. Fold the fish into the flour-based mixture
5. Toss the anchovies into the barrel of the air fryer
6. Switch to the 'air crisp' function at the same temperature for 8-10 minutes
7. Retrieve the crispy anchovies and divide them into 4 portions with 1 wedge of lime per plate

Classic British Jacket Potato (Tuna-Mayo filling)

Prep time: 5 minutes

Cook time: 50 minutes

Serves 4

You've already learnt about the British origins of the jacket potato, but you must try it with the tuna, mayo and sweetcorn filling, which makes it delicious and nutritious for a lunch time meal

Ingredients

- 4 large potatoes
- 60g butter (4 tbsp)
- 1 tsp ground black pepper (optional)
- 1 tsp chilli flakes (optional)
- 2 tins of tuna chunks in brine (370g)
- 4 tbsp mayonnaise
- 100g sweetcorn

Preparation Instruction

1. Preheat the air fryer at 180° for 5 minutes
2. Make multiple insertions in the potato with a fork, ensuring they do not burst whilst baking
3. Place the potatoes into the air fryer and select the 'bake/roast' function at 200° for 50 minutes
4. Meanwhile, open the tuna cans and scoop the tuna into mixing bowl
5. Add 4 tbsp of mayonnaise and stir thoroughly to form a paste like mixture
6. Toss in the sweet corn and mix once again
7. Retrieve the potatoes and cut down the centre of the potatoes
8. Plate the potatoes up and layer a tbsp of butter in the centres
9. Divide the tuna-mayo mixture by 4 and dollop it in the centre of each potato
10. Season the potatoes with ground black pepper and chilli flakes (optional)

Fishcakes with Lemon

Prep time: 10 minutes

Cook time: 10-12 minutes

Serves 2

A very simple dish that can serve as a quick snack or appetiser. Fishcakes are very soft from the inside and can be crispy from the outside when done properly.

Ingredients

- 300g finely chopped white fish (any)
- 15g finely chopped coriander
- 2 lemon wedges (½ a Lemon)
- 30g mayonnaise
- 2 tbsp sweet chilli sauce
- 80g of dried breadcrumbs

- 1 large egg
- 1/8 tsp sea salt
- ½ tsp ground pepper
- 1cal olive oil fry spray

Preparation Instructions

1. Spay the barrel of the air fryer generously, using 1cal fry spray
2. Preheat the air fryer at 180°C for 4-5 minutes
3. Using a mixing bowl, amalgamate the fish, coriander, egg, mayo, and sweet chilli sauce by hand mixing or stirring with a fork
4. Hand shape the mixture into fish cakes
5. Place the fishcakes in the air fryer and select the 'grill' setting at 200°C for 10-12 minutes (if applicable to your machine)
6. Retrieve the fishcakes and divide them by 2
7. Serve with the lime wedges

Tandoori Cod Sandwich

Prep time: 25 minutes
Cook time: 15-30 minutes
Serves 2
This dish is an amalgamation of the east and west, and is certainly accepted in British culinary cuisine. A crispy tandoori cod sandwiched in between tasty pickle, onion, and wholemeal bread.

Ingredients

- 25g tandoori masala
- 50ml olive oil
- 55g Greek yogurt
- 150g Cod fillets x2
- 2 sliced pickles
- 2 slices of red onion
- 4 slices of Wholemeal bread
- 1/8 tbsp sea salt
- 1/8 tbsp ground black pepper

Preparation Instructions

1. Preheat the air fryer at 180°C for 5 minutes
2. Within a mixing bowl, combine ¾ of the olive oil, all of the tandoori masala, 1/3 of the Greek yogurt, and salt using a fork
3. Dip the cod pieces into this mixture and coat well
4. Use the rest of the oil to grease bottom part of the air fryer barrel

5. Set the air fryer to the 'grill' setting at 180°C for 8-10 minutes

6. Place the cod pieces into the air fryer and flip half way through the cooking duration

7. Retrieve the cod fillets and set them aside

8. Place the bottom layer of the bread on a plate and top with a slice of red onion

9. Top the red onion with the tandoori cod fillet

10. Finalise the filling with the sliced pickle

11. Create a sandwich by putting a slice of bread on the top of the fish

Ahi Tuna with Green Beans & Vegetable Puree

Prep time: 15 minutes
Cook time: 15 minutes
Serves 2

We love embracing different cultures and cuisines, where Japanese food is definitely a 'go to'. Ahi tuna is cold seared tuna that can be served with a delicious side of aromatised green beans and Vegetable-based Puree. This meal can be eaten with chop sticks or a fork.

Ingredients

• 200g seared ahi tuna (16-18 slices)

For Puree

• 50g cauliflower florets
• 80g carrots
• 1 sliced garlic clove
• ½ tsp minced ginger
• 1 tbsp sesame oil
• ¾ teaspoon sea salt

For Sesame Green Beans

• 125g green beans
• ½ tsp Sesame oil
• ½ tsp olive oil
• 1 tsp minced garlic
• ½ tsp minced ginger
• 1 tbsp water
• 1 tsp soy sauce
• ¼ tsp sesame seeds
• 25g grated carrots
• 25g red cabbage
• 2 tbsp coriander leaves
• 1 tbsp thin sliced green onions

Preparation Instructions

1. Remove the tuna from the packet and place it in the refrigerator for 2-3hrs

2. Steam all of the 'For Puree' vegetables in the air fryer for 12 minutes if applicable to your machine, or boil them on the stove

3. Retrieve the vegetables, toss them into a blender and blend until the ingredients transform into a paste

4. Set the puree aside

5. Add the oils from the 'for sesame green beans' ingredients into the air fryer to warm

6. Select the 'sear/sauté' function on the air fryer and toss in the garlic and ginger for 45 seconds

7. Stir these ingredients and add green beans

8. After the 1 minute mark pour in the water and soya sauce
9. Allow all of these ingredients to sear and aromatise for 3-4 minutes
10. Retrieve the green beans and divide them into two plates
11. Top with the additional grated carrot and cabbage, coriander, and onions (optional)
12. Divide the puree in two and plot it on the plates
13. Take the seared ahi tuna out if the fridge, and divide them by 2
14. Place the seared ahi tuna slices symmetrically along the puree and serve
15. Sprinkle the tuna and green beans with sesame seeds

Salmon and Spinach Risotto

Prep time: 15 minutes
Cook time: 20 minutes
Serves 4
Salmon and Spinach Risotto is a low carbohydrate dish packed with nutrients and flavour. Although the dish has Italian origins, it is well accepted in great Britain, and can serve as a great main course.

Ingredients

- 4 x 113g smoked salmon fillets
- 1 tsp ground black pepper
- 55g unsalted butter
- 75g chopped onion
- 300g cauliflower head
- 125ml fish stock
- 20g parmesan cheese
- 1 tsp sea salt
- 2 tbsp chopped dill
- 225g chopped spinach
- 1 chopped celery stalk
- 2 chopped garlic cloves
- 75g double cream

Preparation Instructions

1. Preheat the air fryer at 180°C for 5 minutes
2. Dash salt and pepper on the salmon fillets, followed by 1 tbsp of dill
3. Toss half of the butter into the barrel of the air fryer
4. Select the 'sear/sauté' in the 'high-medium' setting
5. After 3-4 minutes, the butter should be melted, so place the salmon fillets on top
6. Sear the salmon for 4 minutes
7. Flip the salmon and switch the air fryers setting to 'bake/roast' at 180°C for 6-8 minutes, creating flaky salmon fillets
8. At the 4 minutes mark of baking, dollop in the remainder of the butter, smothering the salmon fillets
9. Once you retrieve the salmon, cover it in foil to keep it warm
10. Remove the barrel again
11. Revert to the air fryers 'sear/sauté' function for around 10 minutes on a medium heat and add spinach, onion, celery

12. At the 2 minute mark, add cauliflower
13. After another 3 minutes, pour in the fish stock, then toss in the garlic and dill
14. Leave the ingredients to sear for another 5 minutes, allowing the liquid to evaporate
15. To finalise the spinach risotto, include double cream in to the mix and stir
16. Divide the risotto and dollop it on 4 plates
17. Place a salmon fillets each portion of risotto

Simple Minced Fish Pots

Prep time: 5 minutes
Cook time: 10 minutes
Serves 2
So you don't like the effort of preparing a food? No problem, we've got you. The simple minced fish pot offers a healthy protein-packed meal without difficult preparation. All you need to do is combine 4 simple ingredients and pop it in the air fryer.

Ingredients

- 500g minced fish or lobster
- ¼ tsp sea salt
- ¼ tsp ground black pepper
- 30g chopped coriander
- ½ an onion
- 2 tbsp pre prepared lemon and garlic butter

Preparation Instructions

1. Simply hand mix the 4Ingredients
2. Toss the fish mince into the air fryer
3. Select the 'pressure' setting on 'high' for 7-8 minutes
4. Take the cooked mince out of the air fryer and divide it into two bowls
5. Dollop a tbsp of the lemon and garlic butter into each bowl of fish (optional)

Healthy Fish Supper

Prep time: 5 minutes
Cook time: 10-11 minutes
Serves 2
Supper is a light British meal eaten a few hours after dinner (5-9pm). The supper meal is not that common, but if you ever feel peckish, why not try our 'healthy fish supper'.

Ingredients

- 200g skinned white fish fillets (2 fillets)

- 100g chopped sausage (meat of choice)
- 30g chopped parsley
- 40ml lemon juice
- 1 tbsp olive oil
- 1 tin drained Lima beans

Preparation Instructions

1. Tip the Lima beans into the air fryer using the 'bake/roast' setting for 5 minutes
2. After the 5 minute duration, pour in half the lemon juice and oil, all of the sausage and half of the parsley
3. The next step would be to lay the fish on top of these ingredients and then drizzle the remainder of the oil
4. Reset the air fryer and cook the ingredients for another 5-6 minutes
5. Retrieve the ingredients, divide into 2 and plate them up

Trout With Chinese Vegetables

Prep time: 5 minutes
Cook time: 20 minutes
Serves 2
Trout is an easily accessible fish in the UK. Combined with all of the seasoning and vegetables, the fish makes for a delicious low-calorie meal.

Ingredients

- 2 x 250g whole trout
- For fish stuffing
- ½ peeled and matchstick-shape sized ginger
- 8 thin sliced bulbs of spring onion
- 100g thinly sliced mange trout
- 400 grams of peeled/sliced carrot
- 2 tbsp Worchester sauce
- 1 tsp sesame oil
- 30g chopped coriander

Preparation Instructions

1. Start by preheating the air fryer at 180° for 3-5 minutes
2. Meanwhile, mix all of the 'for fish stuffing' ingredients in a medium sized bowl
3. Divide the stuffing by 2 and place half inside the cavity of the fish and the other half outside
4. Place the fish on a cooking tray and place them in the air fryer at 180° for 20 minutes, or the 'grill' setting (if applicable)
5. Remove the fish from the air fryer, plate up the 2nd half of the Chinese vegetable on a plate

6.Place the fish on top of the Chinese vegetable and serve

Prawn Pie Pots

Prep time: 5 minutes
Cook time: 10 minutes
Serves 4-5
A close variation to the traditional steak and kidney beans pie, but we have opted tasty prawn cocktail filling.

Ingredients
- 500g prawn filler
- 1 sheet puff pastry
- 1cal olive oil fry spray
- 1 beaten egg

Preparation Instructions
1.Preheat the air fryer to 180° for 5-6 minutes
2.Meanwhile, cut out ramekin shaped pastry
3.Spray 4 ramekins thoroughly using the fry spray
4.Fill the ramekins with prawn filler and cover with the pastry (You can also layer of the bottom of the ramekins with pastry if preferred)
5.Make a small incisions at the centre of the pastry
6.Brush over the top of the pastries with the beaten egg
7.Place the patties in the air fryer for 10-12 minutes at 180°C
8.Retrieve the prawn pie pots and serve

Masala Fish

Prep time: 10 minutes
Cook time: 10 minutes
Serves 4
A simple spicy fish, best cooked on the 'air crisp' setting as the original recipe is deep fried.

Ingredients
- 500g white fish fillets (125g x 4)
- 2 tsp sea salt
- 1 ½ tsp turmeric Powder
- 1 ½ tsp coriander
- 2 tsp tandoori

Preparation Instructions

1. Start by preheating the air fryer at 180°C for 4-5 minutes
2. Place all of the spice powders into a small bowl
3. Rub the spice mix onto the fish thoroughly
4. Place the fish in the air fryer for 10 minutes
5. Retrieve the masala fish and serve

Spicy Fish Balls

Prep time: 10 minutes

Cook time: 10 minutes

Serves 2

This recipe is similar to a fish cake, but much more spicy and smaller, making them the perfect bite size starters.

Ingredients

- 300g finely chopped catfish
- 80g panko bread crumbs
- 50g finely chopped coriander
- 30g chilli mayonnaise
- ½ finely diced red chilli
- ½ finely diced green chilli
- 1 large egg
- 1Cal fry spray
- 1/8 sea salt

Preparation Instructions

1. Spray the barrel of the air fryer thoroughly
2. Preheat the air fryer to 180°C for 5 minutes
3. Meanwhile, using a large mixing bowl, combine the fish, bread crumbs, chilli, chilli mayo, salt, coriander and egg
4. Fold and combine the ingredients thoroughly with your hands
5. Hand mould 8 small fish balls and place them into the air fryer
6. Cook the spicy fish balls for 7-10 minutes
7. Remove the spicy fish balls from the air fryer and serve

Burger Sliders

Prep time: 20 minutes
Cook time: 10-12 minutes
Serves 16
The very western burger slider makes the perfect appetiser for any party or large gathering, serving up to 16 people. The burger slider is a tasty hand made burger sandwiched in-between mini wholemeal buns.

Ingredients
Mini Burgers
- 600g lamb mince
- 30g chopped coriander
- 1 large egg yolk
- 1 tbsp flaxseed oil
- ¼ tsp of Himalayan salt
- ¼ tsp of ground black pepper
- 1 tbsp dijon mustard

To serve/condiments
- 16 quarter slices of British mature cheddar
- 16 quarter sliced beef tomato
- 16 tsp of tomato ketchup or BBQ sauce
- ½ shredded lettuce
- 16 mini wholemeal buns
- 16 mini wooden flat paddles

Preparation Instructions
1. Mix all of the 'burger' ingredients in a mixing bowl and shape up into 16 mini burger patties a quarter the size of your palm
2. Preheat the air fryer at 180°C for 4-5 minutes
3. Place the burger patties in the barrel of the air fryer
4. Select the air fryers 'grill' setting
5. Leave the burgers for 10-12 minutes
6. Flip the burgers at the half way point of the selected cooking time
7. Place the bottom layer of the bun on a plate
8. In order, top the bun with lettuce, sliced tomato, burger patty, cheese, 1 tsp of preferred sauce
9. Place the top layer of the bun on the burger

10.Penetrate the mini wooden flat paddle in the centre of the burger to help hold it together

Spicy Lamb Skewers

Prep time: 10 minutes

Cook time: 20-25 minutes

Serves 3

A very simple lamb skewer recipe, but with just the right amount of seasoning. This is more of a middle eastern type of dish, but the flavours are perfect for British taste buds. The variation of vegetables offer lots of fibre and micronutrients, making it a 'healthy' recipe.

Ingredients

- 12 large cube-shapes lamb chunks (600g)
- ¼ tsp sea salt
- ¼ tsp chilli flakes
- 1 crushed garlic clove
- 1 red pepper
- 1 orange bell pepper
- 1 onion
- 1 tbsp olive oil
- ¼ tsp ground black pepper
- 1 tbsp unsalted butter
- 1 tbsp rosemary
- 1 green pepper
- ½ a courgette
- 30g finely diced coriander

Preparation Instructions

1.Combine all of the ingredients by rubbing them into the meat
2.Refrigerate the meat for 6-24hrs, allowing for the flavours to infuse
3.Prior to cooking the lamb pieces, pre-heat the air fryer to 180°C for 4-5 minutes
4.Chop the vegetables into bite-size chunks
5.Select the air fryers 'steam' setting for 10 minutes and toss in the vegetables
6.Change the setting to 'grill' and place the lamb in for another 10 minutes at 200°C
7.Retrieve the food items, then divide them into 3
8.Pierce 4 chunks of meat and the veg onto each wooden skewer (x3); making sure no food items are pierce twice correspondingly for aesthetic purposes
9.Garnish the skewers with the diced coriander and serve

Peri Peri Chicken Sandwich

Prep time: 15 minutes

Cook time: 20 minutes

Serves 4

The peri peri chicken sandwich has become a British favourite ever since the establishment of the Nando's restaurant starting in 1992 and the influx from the 21st century. This is not a Nando's recipe, but our take on a good peri peri chicken sandwich that should satisfy your taste buds.

Ingredients

- 4 Large chicken breasts
- For Marinade
- 2 tbsp coconut oil
- 1 tsp peri peri salt
- To Serve
- 4 American cheese slices
- 4 cut white floured buns
- 50ml balsamic vinegar
- ¾ of a bottle of peri peri marinade (flavour optional)
- 300g Greek yogurt
- 4 tbsp of mayonnaise

Preparation Instructions

1. Mix all of the ingredients into a bowl except the chicken, cheese and bap to make a marinade
2. Place the chicken breasts in between 2 plastic wraps and mash with the meat tenderiser
3. Submerge the chicken in the marinade and rub thoroughly
4. Apply clingfilm on top of the bowl and refrigerate for 6-24hrs, allowing the chicken to marinate
5. Pre-heat the air fryer for 5 minutes at 180°C
6. Select the 'grill' setting and place the chicken breasts into the air fryer for 20 minutes for a crispy texture
7. Heat up the baps (optional), spread 1 tbsp of mayonnaise on the bottom layer of baps
8. Place a slice of American cheese on the top layers of the baps
9. Take the peri peri chicken breast out of the air fryer and sandwich them in-between the baps

Meatball Sub

Prep time: 5 minutes
Cook time: 14 minutes
Serves 4
The perfect sub for lunch. The 6" sub contains meatballs covered in marinara sauce and cheese, with a dash of coriander.

Ingredients

For meatballs

- 10 medium sized meat balls
- 30g grated mature cheddar
- 4 seeded 6" subs
- 30g finely diced coriander

For marinara sauce

- 30g Tomato Ketchup
- 1 tsp Chopped Garlic
- 1 Tsp Basil
- 1/8 tsp Sea Salt
- 1 Can Tinned Tomatoes
- 1 Tsp Parsley
- 2 Tsp Oregano
- 1/8 tsp Pepper

Preparation Instructions

1. Preheat the air fryer at 180°C for 3-4 minutes
2. Place the meatballs in the air fryer for 8 minutes

3. Toss all of the 'for marinara sauce' ingredients into a blender and blend
4. Retrieve the meatballs and slice them in half, creating 20 halves
5. Place the meatballs in a bowl and pour the tomato sauce over them, then fold them using a wooden spoon
6. Air fry the subs for 4 minutes at 180°C
7. Load up each sub with 5 meatballs halves and top with cheese
8. Dash the coriander on the opening of the sub and serve

Peri Peri Strip Salad

Prep time: 15 minutes
Cook time: 20 minutes
Serves 4
The peri peri strip salad is a tasty, yet low calories compared to the peri peri chicken sandwich, due to having a lower carbohydrate and fat content.

Ingredients
- 4 Large chicken breasts

Salad
- 1 diced lettuce
- ½ diced purple cabbage
- 1 diced beef tomato
- 50g rocket
- 1 grated carrot

For Marinade
- 50ml balsamic vinegar
- 2 tbsp coconut oil
- ¾ of a bottle of peri peri marinade (flavour optional)
- 1 tsp peri peri salt
- 300g Greek yogurt

To Serve
- 4 tbsp garlic and herb salad dressing

Preparation Instructions
1. Mix the 'for marinade' ingredients in a bowl to make the marinade
2. Place the chicken breasts in between 2 plastic wraps and mash with the meat tenderiser
3. Slice each chicken breast into 4 strips
4. Submerge the chicken in the marinade and rub thoroughly
5. Apply clingfilm on top of the bowl and refrigerate for 6-24hrs, allowing the chicken to marinate
6. Pre-heat the air fryer for 5 minutes at 180°C
7. Select the 'grill' setting and place the chicken breasts into the air fryer for 20 minutes for a

crispy texture

8. Divide the salad into 4 plates and top with garlic and herb dressing

9. Take 4 peri peri strips, place then on top of each salad bowl and serve

Grilled Marinara Mince & Cheese Sandwich

Prep time: 5 minutes

Cook time: 14 minutes

Serves 4

A tasty but sloppy sandwich. This sandwich contains marinara mince and 2 cheeses sandwiches in-between tasty wholemeal bread.

Ingredients

For lamb mince

- 500g lamb mince
- 8 seeded wholegrain slices of bread
- 30g grated mature cheddar
- 30g parmesan cheese

For marinara sauce

- 30g Tomato Ketchup
- 1 Can Tinned Tomatoes
- 1 tsp Chopped Garlic
- 1 tsp Parsley
- 1 tsp Basil
- 2 tsp Oregano
- 1/8 tsp Sea Salt
- 1/8 tsp Pepper

Preparation Instructions

1. Preheat the air fryer at 180°C for 3-4 minutes
2. Place the lamb mince in the air fryer for 8 minutes
3. Meanwhile, toss all of the 'for marinara sauce' ingredients into a blender and blend
4. Retrieve the mince meat
5. Toss the mince meat in a bowl and pour over tomato sauce
6. Continue folding the mince meat into the sauce for 2-3 minutes
7. Spread the parmesan on 4 slices of bread,
8. Place all of the bread in the air fryer for 3 minutes
9. Retrieve all the bread
10. Place the cheese topped bread on a plate and load it up with the lamb mince
11. Top the mince with cheddar
12. Repeat this process with all of the sandwiches, then serve

Kentucky Air Fried Chicken Wings

Prep time: 10 minutes

Cook time: 30 minutes

Serves 4

Kentucky fried chicken wings make for a great appetiser or as part of a main dish. This recipe is a healthier variant of the deep fried variant

Ingredients

- 1400g of chicken wings (15-16 wings)
- 2 large eggs
- 3 tsp paprika
- 2 tsp onion powder
- 1 tsp ground black pepper
- 350ml buttermilk
- 240g all-purpose flour
- 2 tsp garlic powder
- 2 tsp salt
- 1cal olive oil spray

Preparation Instructions

1. Preheat the air fryer at 180°C for 3-4 minutes
2. Amalgamate the buttermilk and eggs in a stand mixer
3. Using a small bowl, combine all of the dry ingredients to make the coating flour
4. Employing some kitchen tongs, submerge each chicken wings in the flour, followed by the buttermilk, then back into the flour
5. Place the chicken in the air fryer and cover it with the fry spray
6. Preferably select the 'air crisp' function or cook the chicken at 180°C for 20 minutes
7. Shake the chicken wings and cook for another 5 minutes
8. Retrieve the chicken wings and place them into a dish, then serve

Beef Jerky

Prep time: 10 minutes

Cook time: 120

Serves 4

Beef jerky is the perfect salty snack that can be eaten on the go and at any time of the day.

Ingredients

- 500g thinly sliced beef (sirloin)
- 120ml Worchester Sauce
- 120ml Soy Sauce
- 1 tbsp honey
- 1 tsp onion powder

Preparation Instructions

1. Using a medium sized bowl, mix the sauces and powders to create a marinade
2. Add the beef Jersey into the sauce
3. Cover the bowl with clingfilm and refrigerate the food content for 4-24hrs, allowing the flavours to infuse with the meat
4. Retrieve the food content and drain the beef from any excess fluid using a sieve
5. Preheat the air fryer to 180°C for 3-4 minutes
6. Place the beef Jersey in the barrel if the air fryer
7. Apply the slow cook setting for 2hrs or set the temperature to 100°C for 2hrs
8. You can add a some water every hour to keep the beef moist and prevent burning
9. Retrieve the beef Jersey and set aside to cool
10. Divide by 4 and serve

Beef Chapli Kebab Pita

Prep time: 15 minutes
Cook time: 15 minutes
Serves 4
A milder variant of the South Asian beef chapli kebab, sandwiched into pockets of pita, salad and yogurt/mint sauce.

Ingredients

For Kebab

- 500g beef mince
- ½ a white onion
- 1 tbsp of fresh mint
- 2 tsp ground coriander
- 1 tsp of flaxseed oil
- 1 large egg
- 1 green chilli
- 1 tsp ground cumin
- 2 crushed garlic cloves

For Pita

- 4 pita breads
- ½ diced lettuce
- 1 Sliced tomato
- 60g mint and yogurt sauce

Preparation Instructions

1. Preheat the air fryer at 180°C for 4-5 minutes
2. Hand mix all of the ingredients together in a medium sized bowl, except for the oil
3. Hand mould 4-5 thin palm-size kebab patties
4. Brush the chapli kebabs with olive oil
5. Place the chapli kebabs in the air fryer for 15 minutes at 200°C
6. Retrieve the chapli kebabs using cooking tongs and cut then in half

7. Cut the pita in half and fill quarter of the pockets with lettuce
8. Place half a kebab in each pocket, followed by a slice of tomato
9. Top the pita halves with mint and yogurt sauce, then serve

Sweet and Sour Pork With Rice

Prep time: 30 minutes
Cook time: 25 minutes
Serves 4
Sweet and sour pork is a very oriental dish, but is enjoyed by British people across the country. The dish is very sweet/sticky and well complimented with a small side of a savoury variant of rice.

Ingredients

Pork
- 450g boneless porn shoulder (or substitute)
- 1 tsp sesame oil
- 1 egg
- 2 tbsp soy sauce
- ½ tsp garlic granules
- 30g crushed cornflakes

Sauce
- 75g tomato ketchup
- 45g rice vinegar
- 1 tsp sea salt
- 160ml water
- 45g honey
- 1 tbsp sambal oelek
- ½ tsp paprika
- ¾ tsp corn starch

Additional sides and condiments
- 50g sesame seeds
- 250g ready egg rice

Preparation Instructions

1. Chop the meat into 1" cubes
2. Begin marinating the meat by placing it in a medium sized
3. Add ½ tbsp, 1 tsp sesame oil, and ½ tsp garlic granules
4. Hand rub the marinade on the meat and then set it aside
5. To make the sauce, add and mix the following ingredients; ketchup, honey, vinegar, sambal, salt, paprika and 130ml of water
6. In a separate small bowl, stir together 30ml of water and the corn starch
7. Beat the egg into another small bowl and then mix it with the marinated meat
8. Coat the meat with the cornflakes and set it aside
9. Preheat the air fryer at 180°C for 5 minutes
10. Place the meats in the air fryer and cook them for 5 minutes
11. Retrieve the meat and set aside
12. Pour the sauce into the air fryer and heat up for a minute
13. Add the corn starch to the mix and stir
14. Leave the ingredients to cook for 3 minutes

15. Transfer the sauce on top of the meat and mix thoroughly
16. Dash the sesame seeds on top of the meat, divide the meat on 4 plates and then set aside
17. Cook the egg fried rice in the air fryer at 180°C for 5-6 minutes
18. Remove the rice and divide it on the plates before serving

Greek Pork Chops

Prep time: 10 minutes
Cook time: 5-7 minutes
Serves 4

Ingredients

- 4 pork chops
- 2 tbsp avocado oil
- 1 tbsp fresh chopped rosemary
- 4 grated garlick cloves
- 1 tsp sea salt
- ¼ tsp ground black pepper
- 30ml lemon juice

Preparation Instructions

1. Using a large bowl, add the avocado oil, garlic and rosemary, then stir into a marinade
2. Cover the pork chops with this marinade
3. Cover the bowl with clingfilm and refrigerate the lamb chops 6-24hrs, allowing the flavours to infuse with the meat
4. Preheat the air fryer at 200°C for 4-5 minutes
5. Sprinkle the sea salt and ground pepper around the pork chops
6. Place the pork chops into the air fryer and
7. Set the air fryer at 200°C for 5-7 minutes
8. Retrieve the pork chops and plate then up
9. Squirt lemon juice over the pork chops and serve

Grilled Ham & Cheese Sandwich

Prep time: 2 minutes
Cook time: 8 minutes
Serves 4

Ingredients

- 8 slices of bread

- 8 pieces of deli ham (meat of choice)
- 115g of thin chopped cheddar cheese
- 4 tbsp of olive margarine
- 4 tablespoons of mayonnaise or mustard

Preparation Instructions

1. Preheat the air fryer at 180°C for 5-6 minutes
2. Spread 1 tbsp of margarine for every 2 slices of bread
3. Place the bread in the air fryer
4. Spread the cheese across the bread
5. Add the deli ham and dollop 1tbsp of mayonnaise on the meat
6. Place the second layer of bread on top of the deli meat to create a sandwich
7. Air fry the sandwiched for 6-8 minutes at 200C and slip the sandwich at the half way point
8. Retrieve the sandwiches and plate them up to serve

Air Fried Sausages and Potato

Prep time: 15 minutes
Cook time: 20 minutes
Serves 4

Ingredients

- 1 kg potatoes
- 400g/6 British sausages (meat of choice)
- 1 onion
- 30ml olive oil
- 1 tbsp all-purpose seasoning
- ½ tbsp garlic granules
- 1/8 tsp sea salt
- 1/8 tsp ground black pepper

Preparation Instructions

1. Preheat the air fryer at 200°C for 8 minutes
2. Meanwhile, peel and dice the potatoes into small cubes
3. Wash the potatoes under cold running water, using a sieve
4. Toss the potatoes into a large bowl
5. Hand mix with the 4 seasonings (garlic, salt, pepper, all-purpose) and 1 tbsp of olive oil
6. Now toss the potatoes in the air fryer at 180°C for 10 minutes
7. Meanwhile, chop the British sausages into chunks and place them in a medium bowl
8. Drizzle the remainder of the oil on to the sausages
9. Chop up the onion into cubes and add them on top of the Sausages

10. Amalgamate these 2 food products with the potatoes
11. Air fry the sausage and potatoes for another 6-8 minutes
12. Retrieve the sausage and potatoes and divide them by 4 to serve

Meat Pie Pots

Prep time: 5 minutes
Cook time: 15 minutes
Serves 4
Meat Pie or Pukka pie is a national British food that you can pick up at the fish & Chips shop, or better make your own in the air fryer. It's traditionally made from left over steak meat, and layered of baked pastry.

Ingredients

- 500g cooked steak meat
- 1 sheet puff pastry
- 1cal olive oil fry spray
- 1 beaten egg

Preparation Instructions

1. Preheat the air fryer to 180° for 5-6 minutes
2. Meanwhile, cut out ramekin shaped pastry
3. Spray 4 ramekins thoroughly using the fry spray
4. Fill the ramekins with meat and cover with the pastry (You can also layer of the bottom of the ramekins with pastry if preferred)
5. Make a small incisions at the centre of the pastry
6. Brush over the top of the pastries with the beaten egg
7. Place the patties in the air fryer for 15-17 minutes at 180°C
8. Retrieve the meat pie pots and serve

Air Fryer Bone Marrow

Prep time: 10-15 minutes
Cook time: 10-15 minutes
Serves 4
Ever sucked a beef bone to draw out the gooey, tasty bone marrow? They taste too good to let go to waste. These bones marrows are baked in the air fryer with a layer of paste consisting of garlic, lemon zest, bread crumbs and oil. This recipe makes a great appetiser before a main course

Ingredients

- 2 quartered beef marrow bones (8 pieces)
- 2 ½ cloves grated garlic
- 20g lemon zest
- 60g bread crumbs
- 45ml extra virgin olive oil

Preparation Instructions

1. Preheat the air fryer to 210°C for 8-10 minutes
2. Wash the bones, ensure not to force too much pressure in the cavity, or it could release the marrow
3. Pour 1/3 of the extra virgin olive oil in the air fryer
4. Fold all of the ingredients in a medium sized bowl to crest a 'paste'
5. Dollop this paste at the top of the bone marrow cavity
6. Place the marrows in the air fryer and cook for 10-15 minutes
7. Retrieve the air fried marrows and serve with a tea spoon

Meat Samosas

Prep time: 3 minutes
Cook time: 12 minutes
Serves 6

Samosas are generally considered as a appetiser or snack. With this recipe, you would simply air fry pre prepared samosas. You could pick them up from a supermarket like Sainsbury's. For the more traditional variants, go to the local South Asian corner shop, which are scattered all around the UK.

Ingredients

- 6 meat or lamb mince Samosas
- 1 tbsp olive oil
- 60g chutney (of choice)

Preparation Instructions

1. Preheat the air fryer at 200°C for 5 minutes
2. Remove 6 Samosas from the packet and place them in the barrel of the air fryer
3. Brush oil over the Samosas
4. Cook the Samosas at 180°C for 8-12 minutes
5. Flip the samosas half way whilst cooking
6. Retrieve the Samosas, plate them up and serve with chutney

Stuffed Mushrooms

Prep time: 10 minutes

Cook time: 20 minutes

Serves 5

A great vegetarian-friendly meal that can be served as a main course, as it is packed with vegetables and cheeses, giving it a great nutritional value.

Ingredients

- 10 large white mushrooms
- 15g cheddar cheese
- 15g chopped onion
- 1 chopped plum tomato
- ¼ tsp ground black pepper

- 30g parmesan cheese
- 1 tbsp flaxseed oil
- 150g chopped red bell pepper
- 2 chopped garlic cloves
- ½ tsp Himalayan salt

Preparation Instructions

1. Place a rack attachment into your air fryer if applicable
2. Preheat the air fryer at 200°C for 4-5 minutes
3. Meanwhile, extract and dice the stems of the mushrooms and set aside
4. Prepare the air fryer for the 'sear/sauté' function at the 'medium' heat setting
5. Pour in the olive oil and toss in the mushroom stems, onions, peppers, garlic, tomatoes
6. Allow these ingredients to cool for 5-6 minutes
7. Add salt and pepper to the mixture at the 3 minute mark of sautéing
8. Retrieve this mixture to fill the mushroom caps as equally as possible, using a tbsp
9. Now select the air fryers 'bake/roast' function at 200°C for 15 minutes, if applicable
10. Gently place the mushrooms into the barrel , ensuring the filling does not fall out
11. Bake the mushrooms for 10 minutes, top with parmesan and cheddar cheese
12. Bake the mushrooms for another 5 minutes, retrieve and serve (2 per person)

Sweet Potato Fries

Prep time: 5 minutes

Cook time: 35 minutes

Serves 2

Air fried sweet potato fries are a 'healthy' and nutrient dense alternative to the deep fried white potatoes. Not to mention, there are vegetarian and even vegan friendly.

Ingredients

- 2 Large Sweet potatoes
- ½ tbsp flaxseed oil
- 1 tsp BBQ seasoning
- ½ tsp mixed herbs
- ½ tsp Himalayan salt
- 2 Tbsp tomato ketchup

Preparation Instructions

1. Preheat the air fryer at 180°C for 3-4 minutes
2. Meanwhile, peel and chop the sweet potato into thin sweet potato fries
3. Toss the potato in a medium sized bowl and add all of the otherIngredients
4. Hand mix the potato to combine the seasoning
5. Place the potato in the barrel of the air fryer and select the 'air crisp' function (if applicable to your model) at 180°C for 10-15 minutes
6. Remove the Fries from the air fryer and divide them into 2 plates to serve
7. Dollop 1 tbsp of tomato ketchup onto each plate (optional)

Corn Hot Dogs

Prep time: 5 minutes

Cook time:25 minutes

Serves 4

The recipe is almost identical to the real, but it uses a vegetarian friendly corn based hot dog. I've been told you can't tell the difference between them.

Ingredients

- 4 corn sausages
- 4 pre-cut wholemeal hot dog buns
- 1 diced red onion
- 4 tbsp dijon mustard
- 4 tbsp tomato ketchup
- 1 Cal fry spray

Preparation Instructions

1. Preheat the air fryer at 180°C for 4-5 minutes
2. Dice and toss the onion into the air fryer while it is heating up
3. Fry spray the barrel of the air fryer
4. Place the corn sausages into the barrel of the air fryer for 10 minutes, at a temperature of 180°C
5. Take the sausages out of the air fryer
6. Remove the corn sausages, but leave the onions for another 10 minutes to caramelise

7. Slide the corn hot dogs into the wholemeal buns
8. Put the onions on top of the corn dogs
9. Dollop 1 tbsp of ketchup and dijon mustard on top of the corn hot dogs and serve

Veggie ¼ Pounder Burger

Prep time: 20 minutes

Cook time: 10-25 minutes

Serves 4

Another replica of the beef ¼ pounder burger. The Veggie ¼ pounder burger is very tasty and full of fibre, which is essential for maintaining good health.

Ingredients

Burger
- 4 corn ¼ Pounder patties

To serve/condiments
- 4 slices of British mature cheddar
- 4 slices red onion
- 4 slices beef tomato
- 4 tbsp of tomato ketchup or BBQ sauce
- ½ of a shredded lettuce
- 4 wholemeal buns
- 4 wooden flat paddles

Preparation Instructions

1. Remove the veg based burgers from the packet
2. Preheat the air fryer at 180°C for 4-5 minutes
3. Place the veg burger patties into the barrel of the air fryer
4. Select the air fryers 'grill' setting (if applicable to your model)
5. Leave the veg burgers to cook for 20-25 minutes
6. Flip the burgers at the half way point of the cooking duration
7. Place the bottom layer of the bun on a plate
8. In order, top the bun with lettuce, sliced tomato, veg burger patty, cheese, 1 tbsp of preferred sauce, and the a slice of red onion
9. Place the top layer of the bun on the burger
10. Penetrate the wooden flat paddle in the centre of the burger to help hold it together
11. Plate up the vegetarian ½ pounder burgers and serve

Corn Chapli Kebabs

Prep time: 15 minutes

Cook time: 15 minutes

Serves 4

This is our twist to the South Asian lamb mince chapli kebab. The kebabs little bit spicy, but the taste buds of many modern day Brits have become accustomed to heat.

Ingredients

- 500g corn mince
- ½ a white onion
- 1 tbsp of fresh mint
- 2 tsp ground coriander
- 1 tsp of flaxseed oil

- 1 large egg
- 1 green chilli
- 1 tsp ground cumin
- 2 crushed garlic cloves

Preparation Instructions

1. Preheat the air fryer at 180°C for 4-5 minutes
2. Hand mix all of the ingredients together in a medium sized bowl, except for the oil
3. Hand mould 4-5 thin palm size kebab patties
4. Brush the corn chapli kebabs with olive oil
5. Place the corn chapli kebabs in the air fryer for 15 minutes at 200°C
6. Retrieve the corn chapli kebabs using cooking tongs and plate them up

Veggie Mince Fajita

time: 15 minutes

Cook time: 15-20 minutes

Serves 4

We have replicated the same Mexican fajita flavour, but with the use of corn mince instead of beef. What's the difference? Well, it's a little bit on the 'healthier' side with a lower fat and much higher fibre content.

Ingredients

- 500g corn mince
- 1 Green pepper
- 1 small red onion
- 1 Packet of fajita seasoning

- 1 Red pepper
- 1 Orange pepper
- 1 tbsp sesame seed oil
- 4 large wholemeal tortillas

Preparation Instructions

1. Pre-heat the air fryer at 180°C for 4-5 minutes

2.Place the corn mince in a large bowl

3.Finely dice the bell peppers and onion, then toss them in with the corn mince

4.Add the fajita mix and then hand mix the ingredients to amalgamate the ingredients

5.Place the corn mixture in the barrel of the air fryer and sprinkle oil

6.Close the air fryer lid and select the set the temperature to 200°C for 15-20 minutes

7.Stir half way through the cooking duration

8.Meanwhile, plate up the tortillas

9.Retrieve the mince and load up the tortillas, ensuring that they are equally filled

10.Wrap the fajitas and serve

Tofu Salad

time: 5 minutes

Cook time: 10 minutes

Serves 4

Tofu is a great alternative to chicken or beef, perfect on a bed of salad, for a healthy and wholesome meal.

Ingredients

- 500g cube cut tofu
- ½ tsp Himalayan salt
- ½ tsp ground black pepper
- 1 tsp smoked paprika
- 1 tbsp Worchester sauce
- 15g corn starch
- ½ tbsp flaxseed oil

Preparation Instructions

1.Preheat the air fryer at 180°C for 3-4 minutes

2.Meanwhile, place all of the 'for tofu' ingredients in a sized medium bowl and hand mix them to infuse the flavours

3.Toss the seasoned tofu into the air fryer at 180°C for 10-15 minutes

4.0While the tofu is cooking, divide the salad in 4 bowls

5.Remove the tofu from the air fryer and place it on top of the salad bowls, then serve

Spicy Tofu Skewers

Prep time: 10 minutes

Cook time: 10 minutes

Serves 3

This recipe is similar to the spicy lamb skewer but with the use of tofu.

Ingredients

For skewer
- 600g cube cut tofu
- 1 courgette
- 1 green pepper
- 1 red pepper
- 1 onion
- 30g finely diced coriander
- 30ml chilli sauce (of choice)

For season
- 1 tbsp olive oil
- ¼ tsp sea salt
- ¼ tsp ground black pepper
- ¼ tsp chilli flakes
- 1 crushed garlic clove

Preparation Instructions

1. Combine all of the 'for season' ingredients by rubbing them into the tofu
2. pre-heat the air fryer to 180°C for 4-5 minutes
3. Chop the vegetables cube shaped chunks
4. Steam the vegetables for 5 minutes
5. Pierce 4 chunks of tofu and the veg onto each wooden skewer (x3); making sure no food items are pierce twice correspondingly for aesthetic purposes
6. Place the skewers in the air fryer at 180°C for 10 minutes
7. Retrieve the skewers and plate them
8. Before serving, drizzle the chill sauce over the skewers, followed by garnishing them with the diced coriander

Sweet Chilli Cauliflower Wings

Prep time: 25 minutes
Cook time: 15-20 minutes
Serves 4
As a vegetarian, you can't have chicken wings, but why not opt for the next best thing. The sweet chilli cauliflower wings are pretty close to chicken, in terms of texture and flavour.

Ingredients
- 850g of cauliflower florets
- 125g all-purpose flour

- 1 tsp baking powder
- 80ml sweet chilli sauce
- 1Cal olive oil fry spray
- ¼ tsp sea salt
- ¼ tsp ground black pepper

Preparation Instructions

1. Preheat the air fryer to 180°C for 4-5 minutes
2. In order to make the batter for the cauliflower wings, mix 150ml of water with flour, baking powder, salt and pepper into a stand mixer
3. Whisk the ingredients and add the cauliflower florets
4. Hand coat the cauliflower florets
5. Fry spray the barrel of the air fryer generously
6. Toss the cauliflower florets into the air at 200°C for 10 minutes
7. Remove the cauliflower wings from the air fryer and pour the sweet chill sauce on top
8. Divide the wings by 4 and serve

Mediterranean Tomatoes

Prep time: 2 minutes
Cook time: 10 minutes
Serves 4
This is a great Mediterranean style recipe for some tasty and juicy tomatoes.

Ingredients

- 4 beef tomatoes
- 1 tbsp olive oil
- 1 ½ tsp Mediterranean spice mix
- 1 tbsp light soy sauce

Preparation Instructions

1. Preheat the air fryer to 180° for 3-4 minutes
2. Slice the beef tomatoes
3. Season the beef tomatoes with the spice mix, soy sauce, and oil
4. Place the tomatoes into the air fryer for 10 minutes
5. Remove the tomatoes from the air fryer and plate them up (1 sliced tomato per plate)

Courgette Chips

Prep time: 5 minutes
Cook time: 10 minutes

Serves 4

These courgette chips are crispy and seasoned well, with additional cheese, for a tasty vegetarian experience.

Ingredients

- 2 Courgettes
- 60g grated veg parmesan cheese
- 1 large egg
- 1/8 tsp sea salt
- 1cal fry spray
- 30g crushed cornflakes
- 35g of all-purpose flour
- 1 tsp all seasons spice mix
- ½ tsp garlic powder

Preparation Instructions

1. Preheat the air fryer to 200°C for 4-5 minutes
2. Peel and chop the courgettes into thick chips, then set aside
3. Using a large sized mixing bowl, mix the cheese, cornflakes, flour, and all of the seasoning
4. Beat an egg into a medium bowl, where you will submerge the courgettes sticks
5. Once the courgettes are covered in egg, dip and coat them with the dryIngredients
6. Place the courgette sticks in the barrel of the air fryer for 10 minutes at the same temperature
7. Retrieve the chips, divide them into 4 portions and plate them up to be served

Mini Vegetarian Sausage Rolls

Prep time: 7 minutes
Cook time: 10 minutes
Serves 9

Ingredients

- 3 Corn Sausages
- 3 sheets of puff pastry
- 1 tbsp sesame seeds
- 1 large egg

Preparation Instructions

1. Preheat the air fryer at 180°C for 7 minutes, whilst preparing the sausage rolls
2. Whisk the large egg in a small bowl
3. Place the puff pastry sheets on a clean flat kitchen surface
4. Place a corn sausage on top of the pastry sheet
5. Roll the pasty around the sausage
6. Lightly brush the pastry with the whisked egg to secure the meat in the pastry
7. Chop the pastry into 3 equal portions to make sausage bites
8. Repeat the process with all of the corn sausages

9. To finalise the corn sausage rolls prior to cooking, Sprinkle the sesame seeds on all of the sausage bites
10. Fry spray the barrel of the air fryer
11. Select the 'bake/roast' setting (if applicable) and place the sausage rolls into the barrel of the air fryer for 10 minutes
12. Take the vegetarian sausage bites out of the air fryer and serve

Daal Served With Pita

Prep time: 5 minutes
Cook time: 25 minutes
Serves 4
Daal is very popular amongst vegetarians across the UK. Daal is a tasty lentil curry that can be served with bread, pita, buns, roti, rice, or simply eaten by spoon.

Ingredients

- 200g lentils (soaked in water for 3hrs)
- 15g butter
- 1 tsp Himalayan salt
- 1 tbsp chilli powder
- 1 tsp dry mango powder
- 8 coriander leaves
- 4 wholemeal pita bread

Preparation Instructions

1. Start by boiling the daal in water over the stove
2. Remove the excess water via a sieve
3. Preheat the air fryer for 12 minutes to 200°C
4. Pour half of the daal into the air fryer for 10 minutes at 200°C
5. At the 3 minute mark, add and stir half of the butter and salt
6. Leave the daal for the remainder 7 minutes
7. Repeat the process with the other half of the daal
8. Add and stir all of the spices (mango, chilli, salt)
9. Pour the daal directly from the air fryer barrel into 4 bowls
10. Place 2 coriander leaves in the middle/top of the daal bowls
11. Plate up the wholemeal pita and serve

Pizza for One

Prep time: 5 minutes
Cook time: 8-10 minutes

Serves 1

A small 6" Pizza is perfect for one. Not all pizzas are suitable for vegetarian, but our recipe cooks a nice 2 cheese and tomato pizza with no meat or chicken products.

Ingredients

- 6" dough whole wheat dough ball
- 2 tbsp tomato sauce
- 40g mozzarella cheese
- 40g cheddar cheese
- 1 tbsp olive oil

Preparation Instructions

1. Preheat the air fryer at 200°C for 4-5 minutes
2. Roll out the dough and place it on a 6" pizza pan
3. Top the dough with tomato sauce and both of the cheeses, ensuring you cover all of the base
4. Place the pizza into the air fryer at 190°C for 8-10 minutes
5. Retrieve the pizza, plate it up and serve

Banana Bread

Prep time: 10 minutes

Cook time: 40 minutes

Serves 10

Sweet banana bread quite possibly has its British origins. It was first baked by housewives during the great depression, between 1929-1939. Our air fryer variant is suitable for vegetarians, or even vegans as it does not contain any animal products.

Ingredients

- 3 Large Mature Bananas
- 90ml avocado oil
- 100g brown sugar
- 225g self-raising flour
- 1 ½ tsp baking powder
- 1 tbsp cinnamon
- 50g dried fruit mix

Preparation Instructions

1. Preheat the air fryer at 200°C for 4-5 minutes
2. Using a large bowl, peel and mash the bananas with a fork, then stir in ¾ of the prepared oil and all of the sugar
3. Add and stir the flour, baking soda, and cinnamon, then toss in the dried fruit

4. Pour the mixture onto a 2lb loaf tin and place it in the air fryer for 20 minutes at 200°C
5. Layer the top with foil and then leave the banana bread in the air fryer for another
6. Retrieve the banana bread and cut 10 slices to serve

Caramelised Pineapple Bakes

Prep time: 6 minutes

Cook time: 13 minutes

Serves 6

The caramelised pineapple bake is the perfect for a snack, appetiser or dessert. It is vegetarian friendly as the main ingredients are fruit and pastry.

Ingredients

- 1 large sheet of puff pasty
- 1 Pineapple
- 2½ tbsp brown sugar
- 30g melted butter
- 1 tsp ground cinnamon

Preparation Instructions

1. Using a sharp knife, remove the skin and seeds from the Pineapple
2. Preheat the air fryer at 180°C for 3 minutes
3. Cut the Pineapple horizontally, into 6 equally sized slices
4. Using a biscuit cutter, extract the core from the Pineapple, creating a ring like shape
5. Put the pineapple slices into a bowl
6. Slice the puff pastry into long think strips
7. Wrap the puff pastry strips around the pineapple rings until the fruit is no longer visible (under the centre cavity and around)
8. Brush over the pineapple pastries with the melted butter
9. Drizzle and massage the brown sugar and cinnamon on the puff pastries
10. Using some kitchen tongs, place the pineapple rings into the air fryer
11. Bake the pineapple at 195°C for 13 minutes, and flipping them at the half way point
12. Once again, using some kitchen tongs, plate the caramelised pineapple rings bakes

Vegetarian Pasta Bake

Prep time: 5 minutes

Cook time: 20 minutes

Serves 2-3

Pasta bakes are a very Italian dish and sometimes with a British twist. They make the perfect main for dinner, with the main ingredients being pasta, cheese and mince.

Ingredients

- 250g corn mince
- 125g diced onions
- ½ diced green bell pepper
- 1/8 tsp sea salt
- 450g plain boiled pasta
- 60g grated cheddar cheese
- 60g shredded corn salami
- 1 tbsp olive oil
- ½ diced red bell pepper
- 1/8 tsp ground black pepper
- 250ml pasta sauce

Preparation Instructions

1. Depending on your air fryer, select the 'sear/saute' function at medium heat or use a stove and pan
2. Start by pouring oil into the barrel of the air fryer for 3-4 minutes
3. Incorporate the onions and bell pepper for 3-4 minutes
4. Toss in the minced corn to brown, and treacle with salt/pepper
5. Dollop the pasta sauce and stir thoroughly
6. Transfer the food content into a baking dish
7. Scatter the corn salami and cheddar on top of the pasta bake ingredients
8. Now set the air fryer to 180°C
9. Place the baking dish in the air fryer and cook for 10-12 minutes
10. Retrieve the pasta bake and serve

Caramelised Apple Bakes

Prep time: 6 minutes
Cook time: 10 minutes
Serves 6

The caramelised apple bake is similar to the pineapple bake, in terms of food category and cooking procedures. However, the caramelised apple bake differs so different in taste and texture. This recipe is also vegetarian friendly, as the main ingredients are fruit and pastry.

Ingredients

- 1 large sheet of puff pasty
- 2 apples
- 2½ tbsp brown sugar
- 30g melted butter
- 1 tsp ground cinnamon

Preparation Instructions

1. Using a peeler, remove the skin of the apples
2. Using a biscuit cutter, remove the core and seeds of the apple

3. Preheat the air fryer to 180°C for 3 minutes
4. Cut the apple horizontally, into 6 equally sized slices (3 slices per apple)
5. Slice the puff pastry into long think strips
6. Wrap the puff pastry strips around the apple rings until the apple is no longer visible (under the centre cavity and around)
7. Brush over the apple pastries with the melted butter
8. Drizzle and massage the brown sugar and cinnamon on the puff pastries
9. Using some kitchen tongs, place the pineapple rings into the air fryer
10. Bake the apple at 195°C for 10 minutes, and flipping them at the half way point
11. Once again, using some kitchen tongs, plate the caramelised apple rings bakes

Aloo & Matar Samosas

Prep time: 3 minutes
Cook time: 12 minutes
Serves 6

Aloo and Matar Samosas are very popular in southern India, but grew in popularity in the UK around the middle of the 20th century. They're considered appetisers and basically consist of chunky spicy potato and peas, fried in a pyramid-shape pastry. These samosas can be picked up from the local South Asian grocery shop, which are scattered all over the UK.

Ingredients

- 6 Aloo and matar filled samosas
- 1 tbsp olive oil
- 60g chutney (of choice)

Preparation Instructions

1. Preheat the air fryer at 200°C for 5 minutes
2. Remove 6 Veg samosas from the packet and place them in the barrel of the air fryer
3. Brush oil over the Veg samosas
4. Cook the Samosas at 180°C for 8-12 minutes
5. Flip the samosas half way whilst cooking
6. Retrieve the Samosas, plate them up and serve with chutney

Cheesy Stuffed Peppers

Prep time: 5 minutes
Cook time: 25-30 minutes
Serves 6

Cream cheese studied peppers make a great starter, which has a soft and smooth filling, yet a crispy outer pepper. A true amalgamation of good flavours.

Ingredients

- 30 mini deseeded pepper halves (all colours)
- 1 tbsp olive oil
- 230g cream cheese
- 85g grated mozzarella cheese
- 2 finely sliced green onions
- ½ tsp garlic powder
- ½ teaspoon sea salt

Preparation Instructions

1. Firstly, preheat the air fryer at 180°C for 5-6 minutes
2. In order to make a cream cheese filling, you must place all of the ingredients (accept peppers) into a stand mixer
3. Whisk the ingredients for 30 seconds
4. Drizzle the oil over the peppers and rub them in thoroughly
5. Load the cavities of the peppers with the cream cheese filling
6. Transfer 8-10 stuffed peppers into the air fryer
7. Select the 'bake/roast' function at 180°C if applicable to your air fryer for 8 minutes
8. Repeat until all of the cheesy stuffed peppers are prepared, then serve

Nachos

Prep time: 5 minutes
Cook time: 5 minutes
Serves 2
Nachos make a great savoury started before dinner or even a snack whilst watching a movie.

Ingredients

- 8 6-inch corn tortillas
- 2 tbsp avocado oil
- ½ teaspoon kosher salt

Preparation Instructions

1. Preheat the air fryer to 180°C for 4-5 minutes
2. Drizzle the oil and salt on the tortillas
3. Cut the tortilla 8 pizza like slices
4. Place the Nachos in the air fryer for 3 minutes (you need cook them in batches)
5. Flip the Nachos and leave them to cook for another 2 minutes
6. Receive the Nachos and serve

Cheesy Pizza Bites

Prep time: 8 minutes
Cook time: 16-20 minutes
Serves 3-4
Pizza has been a family favourite since I could remember. Our air fryer recipe contains all 5 cheeses which really impacts the flavour and texture.

Ingredients

- 8" worth of dough
- 3 tbsp tomato sauce
- 90g mozzarella cheese
- 90g cheddar cheese
- 1 ¼ tbsp olive oil

Preparation Instructions

1. Preheat the air fryer at 200°C for 4-5 minutes

2. Roll out the dough and place it on two 8" pizza pan
3. Top the dough with tomato sauce
4. Sprinkle all of the cheeses on top of the dough
5. Place the pizza into the air fryer at 190°C for 8-10 minutes
6. Remove the pizza and cover with a layer if foil to keep it warm
7. Cut the pizza vertically and then horizontally make small bite size pizza squares, then serve

Quadruple Cheese Stuffed Bell Peppers

Prep time: 5 minutes
Cook time: 25-30 minutes
Serves 4-6
Cream cheese studied peppers make a great starter, which has a soft and smooth filling, yet a crispy outer pepper. A true amalgamation of good flavours.

Ingredients

- 4-6 deseeded top cut bell peppers (all colours)
- 230g cream cheese
- 30g grated cheddar cheese
- 2 finely sliced green onions
- ½ teaspoon sea salt
- 1 tbsp olive oil
- 30g grated mozzarella cheese
- 30g grated parmesan
- ½ tsp garlic powder

Preparation Instructions

1. Firstly, preheat the air fryer at 180°C for 5-6 minutes
2. In order to make a cheese filling, you must place all of the ingredients (accept peppers) into a stand mixer
3. Whisk the ingredients for 30 seconds
4. Drizzle the oil over the peppers and then toss them
5. Load the cavities of the peppers with the filling
6. Transfer all of the stuffed peppers into the air fryer
7. Select the 'bake/roast' function at 180°C if applicable to your air fryer for 8-12 minutes
8. Retrieve the super cheese bell peppers and serve

Cheesy Variety Fries

Prep time: 5 minutes
Cook time: 35 minutes
Serves 2

Ingredients

- 2 Large Sweet potatoes
- 2 Large White potatoes

- 100g cheddar cheese
- ½ tbsp flaxseed oil
- ½ tsp mixed herbs
- 2 Tbsp tomato ketchup
- 100g mozzarella cheese
- 1 tsp BBQ seasoning
- ½ tsp Himalayan salt

Preparation Instructions

1. Preheat the air fryer at 180°C for 3-4 minutes
2. Meanwhile, peel and chop both potatoes into thin fries
3. Toss the potato in a medium sized bowl and add all of the otherIngredients
4. Hand mix the potato to combine the seasoning
5. Place the potato in the barrel of the air fryer and select the 'air crisp' function (if applicable to your model) at 180°C for 8-10 minutes
6. Sprinkle the cheeses on top and cook the chips for another 5-7 minutes
7. Remove the Fries from the air fryer and divide them into 2 plates to serve
8. Spray ketchup over the top of the Fries (optional)

Chilli & Garlic Tandoori Wings

Prep time: 30 minutes

Cook time: 20 minutes

Serves 8

The thigh of the chicken is unique in texture and flavour compared to other cuts like drumsticks, breasts, and wings. Tandoori Chicken has become a British love affair and quite possibly an occasional family favourite.

Ingredients

- 40 chicken wings
- 500g of plain low fat Greek yogurt
- 1/8 tsp of sea salt
- 1cal olive oil fry spray
- 50g finely diced coriander
- 80ml of lemon juice (2 medium lemons)
- 4 tbsp tandoori mix
- 2 mashed garlic cloves
- 5 tbsp chilli garlic sauce

Preparation Instructions

1. Place the chicken wings into a large bowl and add the sea salt and lemon juice
2. Massage these ingredients onto the chicken and create the first coating
3. In a stand mixer, add Greek yogurt, mashed garlic, and tandoori mix
4. Whisk these ingredients until combined, which should form a thick orange coloured tandoori marinade
5. Pour the tandoori marinade onto the wings, massaging around the flesh.
6. Cover the bowl with clingfilm and place it in the refrigerator overnight, allowing the flavours to infuse with the chicken

7. Spay the 1cal fry spray around the barrel of your air fryer
8. Preheat the air fryer at 180°C for 4-5 minutes
9. Using some cooking tongs, place the chicken wings into the barrel of the air fryer and set it to the 'bake/roast' setting at 200°C (if applicable)
10. Leave the chicken wings in the air fryer for around 20 minutes
11. Retrieve the chicken and place them into a large dish
12. Drizzle the chilli garlic sauce over the chicken, or place in separate pots
13. Dash the coriander on top of the chicken and serve

Breaded Air Fried Pickles

Prep time: 5 minutes
Cook time: 8 minutes
Serves 4
The thigh of the chicken is unique in texture and flavour compared to other cuts like drumsticks, breasts, and wings. Tandoori Chicken has become a British love affair and quite possibly an occasional family favourite.

Ingredients

- 38 large pickle slices
- 65g all-purpose flour
- ½ tablespoon water
- ½ teaspoon garlic powder
- ½ teaspoon dried dill
- 130g crushed cornflakes
- 1 large egg
- ½ cup all-purpose flour
- ½ teaspoon paprika
- 1Cal olive oil fry spray

Preparation Instruction

1. Preheat the air fryer to 200°C for 4-5 minutes
2. Employ 3 large bowls
3. In the first bowl add bread crumbs
4. In the second bowl stir egg and water
5. In the third bowl, combine flour, garlic powder, paprika, and dill
6. Submerge the pickles in the flour spice, egg and then coat in the panko bread crumbs
7. Spray the air fryer thoroughly
8. Place the coated pickles in the air fryer and cook them for 4 minutes
9. Flip the pickles and leave them for another 3-4 minutes
10. Retrieve the air fryer pickles and serve

Apple Crisps

Prep time: 5 minutes

Cook time: 8 minutes

Serves 2

These apple crisps are crispy with an amalgamation of sweet, spice and sour. They make a great starter for 2, but the recipe can be scales to serve more people.

Ingredients

- 2 apples
- 2 tsp cinnamon
- ½ tsp chilli flakes

Preparation Instruction

1. Wash, peel, remove centre and slice the apples to around 3mm in width
2. Place the apples flat in the dish
3. Sprinkle half of the cinnamon and chilli flakes
4. Flip the apples and sprinkle the other half of the powders
5. Place the apple slices in the air fryer and set the temperature to 180°C for 8-12 minutes
6. Retrieve the apple chips and serve

Hassle Back potatoes

Prep time: 5 minutes

Cook time: 30 minutes

Serves 4

These apple crisps are crispy with an amalgamation of sweet, spice and sour. They make a great starter for 2, but the recipe can be scales to serve more people.

Ingredients

- 4 medium sized potatoes
- ¼ tsp sea salt
- ¼ tsp ground black pepper
- 60g Garlic butter
- 1cal olive oil fry spray

Preparation Instructions

1. Start by preheating the air fryer at 200°C for 5-6 minutes
2. Meanwhile, make thin slices vertically across the potato, but do not cut all the way through
3. Spray the potatoes thoroughly
4. Sprinkle salt and pepper on the potatoes
5. Insert half of the garlic butter at every opening of the potatoes
6. Place the potatoes in the air fryer at 180°C for 15 minutes
7. Toss in the other half of the garlic butter and cook for another 5-10 minutes if required

8.Restricted the hassle back potatoes and serve

Onion Rings

Prep time: 10 minutes
Cook time: 10 minutes
Serves 4
Onion Rings are breaded and air fried rings of onion which are crispy and soft in texture and savoury in flavour.

Ingredients

- 2 large onions
- 2 large eggs
- 200g panko bread crumbs
- ½ tsp onion powder
- 2 tsp sea salt

- 85g all-purpose flour
- 30ml milk
- 1 tsp paprika
- ½ tsp garlic powder

Preparation Instructions

1.Preheat the air fryer at 200°C for 4-5 minutes
2.Dice the unwanted ends of the onion and peel the skin off
3.Slice the rings into multiple 10-12mm pieces
4.Separate the layers of onions to create multiple rings
5.Employ 4 medium sized bowls to for the costing
6.Beat an egg into one of the bowl and pour in milk
7.Add bread crumbs In another
8.In the third bowl, amalgamate all of the flour and seasoning powders (paprika, onion, garlic, salt)
9.Submerge the onion rings in the powder based mixture, followed by the egg mixture
10.The onion rings should be sticky enough to cost with the breadcrumbs
11.Toss the onion rings in the air fryer at 190°C for 10 minutes
12.Flip the onion rings half way through the cooking duration
13.Remove the onion rings from the air fryer using kitchen tongs and serve

Skin On Potato Wedges

Prep time: 10 minutes
Cook time: 10 minutes
Serves 4
Onion Rings are breaded and air fried rings of onion which are crispy and soft in texture and savoury in flavour.

Ingredients

- 3 large potatoes
- ½ tsp sea

Preparation Instructions

1. Preheat the air fryer to 180°C for 3 minutes
2. Without peeling the potatoes, cut thick wedges using a sharp knife
3. Season the potato wedges with salt, hand folding them in a medium sized bowl
4. Toss the potato wedges in the air fryer for 10-15 minutes at 180°C
5. Divide the potato wedges into 3 portions and serve

Spicy Roast Carrots

Prep time: 5 minutes
Cook time: 15 minutes
Serves 5-6
Nachos make a great savoury started before dinner or even a snack whilst watching a movie.

Ingredients

- 500g of carrots
- 1 tbsp avocado oil
- ½ tsp sea salt
- ½ tsp ground black pepper
- 1 tsp red chilli flakes

Preparation Instructions

1. Preheat the air fryer at 180°C for 4-5 minutes
2. Meanwhile, peel the carrot and chop of the ends off
3. Chop the carrots horizontally into 3 chunks
4. Now Slice the carrots vertically into 3 strips per each chunk
5. Toss the carrots strips in the air fryer for 15 minutes
6. Half way through the cooking duration add salt, pepper and chilli flakes, then stir the carrot
7. Retrieve the carrots and serve

Ravioli

Prep time: 5 minutes
Cook time: 6 minutes
Serves 3
Nachos make a great savoury started before dinner or even a snack whilst watching a movie.

Ingredients

- 15 frozen ravioli
- ½ cup butter milk
- ½ cup panko breadcrumbs
- 1cal olive oil fry spray

Preparation Instructions

1. Preheat the air fryer at 180°C for 3 minutes
2. Pour the butter milk in a small bowl
3. Toss the panko breadcrumbs in another small bowl
4. Submerge the ravioli in the butter milk, followed by the panko breadcrumbs
5. Place the ravioli in the air fryer, equally spread apart
6. Set the air fryer to 200°C for and cook the ravioli for 7-10 minutes
7. Retrieve the ravioli and serve

Nacho Cheese

Prep time: 5 minutes
Cook time: 30 minutes
Serves 16
Nacho cheese is an addition to many starter, most if not all of the starters in mentioned in this book. Just try dipping some nachos or skin on potato wedges in some Nacho cheese.

Ingredients

- 60g butter
- 60g all-,purpose flour
- 400ml milk
- 400g grated cheddar cheese
- 1 tsp sea salt

Preparation Instructions

1. Toss the butter in the barrel of the air fryer and set the temperature to 160°C for 5 minutes
2. Add the all-purpose flour and stir with a spoon
3. Allow the flour to cook for around a minute
4. Pour in the milk
5. Transition to 180°C on the air fryer for another 2-3 minutes
6. Sprinkle 100g of cheddar in to the mix and stir until it melts and combines
7. Retrieve the Nacho Cheese and either create a share bowl, or 16 small individual cups

Spiced Sweet Potatoes

Prep time: 10 mins
Cook time: 15 mins
Serves: 4

Ingredients:

- 2 large sweet potatoes
- 1 tsp paprika
- 1 tsp onion powder
- 1 tsp black pepper
- Olive oil
- 1 tsp cumin
- 1 tsp salt

Preparation Instructions:

1. Chop the sweet potatoes into small cubes of about 2 cm.
2. Combine all the spices and seasonings in a bowl and mix.
3. Add the sweet potatoes and a drizzle of olive oil to the seasoning mix.
4. Stir well and ensure sweet potatoes are covered with spices.
5. Spray air fryer basket with some oil.
6. Add the sweet potato mix to the basket and cook in the air fryer at 200°C for 15 minutes. Shake the basket and spray more oil often to ensure crisp and even sweet potatoes.

Crispy Green Beans

Prep time: 10 mins
Cook time: 10 mins
Serves: 2

Ingredients:

- 200 g green beans
- 15 g grated parmesan cheese
- ½ tsp salt
- 1 tsp garlic powder
- 50 g panko bread crumbs
- 1 egg
- ½ tsp pepper
- Olive oil

Preparation Instructions:

1. In a mixing bowl, combine the breadcrumbs, parmesan, garlic powder and salt and pepper.
2. Beat the egg in a separate bowl.
3. Bread the green beans by first dipping them in the egg mix and then dredging in the

breadcrumb mix.

4.Spray the air fryer basket with olive oil.

5.Arrange the green beans in a single layer in the basket.

6.Cook in an air fryer at 200°C for 5 - 8 minutes; regularly shake the basket to turn green beans.

7.Serve when crispy!

Crispy Chickpeas

Prep time: 5 mins
Cook time: 15 mins
Serves: 2

Ingredients:

- 250 g chickpeas
- ½ tsp garlic powder
- ½ tsp smoked paprika
- ¼ tsp black pepper
- 1 tbsp olive oil

Preparation Instructions:

1.Drain chickpeas and dry them completely. Moisture will prevent the chickpeas from becoming crispy.

2.Put dried chickpeas in an air fryer basket and cook for 12 -15 minutes at a low heat - 90°C.

3.In a mixing bowl, combine spices and olive oil.

4.Mix chickpeas thoroughly with oil and spices.

Crunchy Corn

Prep time: 5 mins
Cook time: 7 mins
Serves: 2

Ingredients:

- 2 ears of corn
- ½ tsp salt
- ½ tsp pepper
- 30 g butter

Preparation Instructions:

1.Melt butter in the microwave or over a low heat.

2.Preheat air fryer to 200°C.

3. Toss the corn in the butter.
4. Season with salt and pepper.
5. Cook in air fryer for 5 minutes.
6. Turn and cook for a further 2 minutes.
7. Serve warm.

Pita Bread Chips

Prep time: <5 mins
Cook time: 8 mins
Serves: 4

Ingredients:

- 4 pitta bread pockets
- 2 tbsp olive oil
- 1 ½ tsp rosemary
- 2 tsp sea salt / rock salt

Preparation Instructions:

1. Cut pita bread into triangles.
2. Mix oil, rosemary and sea salt in a small bowl.
3. Drizzle oil and herbs over pitta breads.
4. Cook pita chips in air fryer at 160°C for 4 minutes.
5. Toss pita chips and cook for a further 4 minutes.

Crispy Kale Chips

Prep time: <5 mins
Cook time: 8 mins
Serves: 4

Ingredients:

- 220 g kale
- 1 tbsp olive oil
- ½ tsp salt

Preparation Instructions:

1. Destalk the kale leaves.
2. Rip the leaves into smaller pieces.
3. Put the kale into a bowl with salt and olive oil.
4. Mix together ensuring kale is covered with salt and oil.

5. Air fry the kale for 4 minutes at 180°C.
6. After 4 minutes, shake the basket and put on to cook for another 2 - 4 minutes. Until the kale is crispy and chip-like.

Cauliflower Wings

Prep time: 5 mins
Cook time: 15 mins
Serves: 2

Ingredients:

- ½ head of cauliflower
- 30 ml Olive Oil
- 120 ml buffalo sauce
- 1 tsp garlic powder
- 1 tsp salt

Preparation Instructions:

1. Cut cauliflower into florets.
2. Stir the buffalo sauce, garlic powder and salt together.
3. Mix the cauliflower with the sauce ensuring all cauliflower is covered.
4. Grease the inside of air fryer basket with some spray oil.
5. Arrange cauliflower florets in the basket ensuring a small gap between each floret.
6. Cook in air fryer for 15 minutes at 180°C.

Halloumi Fries

Prep time: 5 mins
Cook time: 10 mins
Serves: 4

Ingredients:

- 35 g plain flour
- 235 g halloumi cheese
- 1 tsp garlic powder
- Sprinkle of salt and pepper
- Spray oil
- Optional: 1 tsp smoked paprika

Preparation Instructions:

1. Slice halloumi in 1 - 2 cm sticks.

2. Combine garlic, flour, salt and pepper in a bowl.
3. Preheat air fryer to 200°C.
4. Dredge the halloumi in the flour mixture.
5. Arrange halloumi in a single layer in air fryer basket.
6. Cook for 6 - 10 minutes. Until fries are golden.

Stuffed Mushrooms

Prep time: 5 mins
Cook time: 15 mins
Serves: 2

Ingredients:

- 2 portobello mushrooms
- 100 g cream cheese
- 20 g olives
- 20 g sun dried tomatoes
- 30 g grated parmesan

Preparation Instructions:

1. Wash mushrooms and remove stems.
2. Mix cream cheese, olives and sundried tomatoes.
3. Spoon cream cheese mixture into mushroom caps.
4. Evenly sprinkle parmesan on mushroom cups.
5. Cook in air fryer at 200°C for 15 minutes.

Air fryer Olives

Prep time: 5 mins
Cook time: 10 - 12 mins
Serves: 2

Ingredients:

- 20 g plain flour
- 30 g panko bread crumbs
- 1 egg
- 15 g grated parmesan cheese
- 120 g olives

Preparation Instructions:

1. Mix parmesan and bread crumbs together.

2. Prepare a coating station with three bowls - egg in one bowl, flour in another and parmesan bread crumbs in the third bowl.
3. Bread olives by placing them in flour first,then egg and finally breadcrumbs.
4. Air fry at 200°C for 10 - 12 minutes.

Prosciutto Wrapped Asparagus

Prep time: <5 mins
Cook time: 5 mins
Serves: 2

Ingredients:

- 300 g asparagus
- 8 slices prosciutto

Preparation Instructions:

1. Trim asparagus by removing the ends.
2. Wrap each asparagus spear with a slice of prosciutto.
3. Place in air fryer basket and cook at 180°C for 5 minutes.

Perfect Prawns and Vegetables

Prep time: 5 mins
Cook time: 10 mins
Serves: 4

Ingredients:

- 400 g prawns
- 1 red pepper
- 1 onion
- 2 cloves of garlic
- 2 tbsp olive oil
- 1 courgette
- 1 yellow pepper
- 1 lime
- ½ tsp salt
- 2 tbsp cajun seasoning

Preparation Instructions:

1. Marinate prawns in salt, spices, lime juice,garlic and olive oil.
2. Prepare vegetables by dicing them into small cubes
3. Mix prawns and vegetables together.
4. Cook in an air fryer at 200°C for 8 - 10 minutes.

Garlic Bread

Prep time: < 5 mins
Cook time: 5 mins
Serves: 5

Ingredients:

- 5 tbsp butter
- 3 tbsp garlic (minced)
- 50 g parmesan cheese
- French Baguette
- 1 tbsp parsley

Preparation Instructions:

1. Soften butter and mix well with garlic, parsley and parmesan cheese.
2. Slice French baguette and spread garlic butter on each slice.
3. Cook in air fryer at 175°C for 5 minutes.

Sausage Rolls

Prep time: 10 mins
Cook time: 8 - 10 mins
Serves: 4

Ingredients:

- 100 g sausage meat
- 1 sheet of pre prepared puff pastry
- 1 egg
- Optional: 1 tbsp sesame seeds

Preparation Instructions:

1. Preheat air fryer at 180°C for 10 minutes
2. Beat egg in a small bowl.
3. Spread sausage meat in the middle of a sheet of puff pastry.
4. Roll pastry around the sausage meat.
5. Using a pastry brush, brush the egg where the pastry joins.
6. Brush the length of sausage roll with egg.
7. Sprinkle with sesame seeds if using.
8. Cut the stuffed pastry sheet into lengths of 4 cm.
9. Close each end of sausage rolls.
10. Spray air fryer basket with oil.
11. Cook in air fryer for 8 - 10 minutes until the pastry is golden.

Peanut Butter Cookies

Prep time: <5 mins
Cook time: 5 mins
Serves: 20 cookies

Ingredients:

- 175 g Sugar
- 230 g Peanut Butter
- 1 Egg

Preparation Instructions:

1. Line the air fryer basket with some greaseproof paper.
2. Mix the sugar, peanut butter and egg together in a bowl.
3. Using a dessertspoon, scoop spoonfuls of the dough on the greaseproof paper.
4. Use a fork to flatten and mold in cookie shapes.
5. Place the basket in the air fryer at 205°C for 4 - 5 minutes.
6. Allow time for cookies to cool before moving them off greaseproof paper.
7. After some cooling time, place cookies on a wire rack to cool.

Caramelized Banana

Prep time: 5 mins
Cook time: 10 mins
Serves: 2

Ingredients:

- 2 Bananas
- 40 g light brown sugar
- 1 tsp cinnamon
- Choice of topping - whipped cream, ice cream, creme fraiche, custard.

Preparation Instructions:

1. Mix the cinnamon and brown sugar together.
2. Line the air fryer basket with some greaseproof paper.
3. Peel the bananas and place them on the greaseproof paper.
4. Evenly sprinkle the cinnamon sugar mixture over the bananas.

5. Place the bananas in the air fryer at 205°C for 8 - 10 minutes.

6. When the topping is caramelized and bubbling, you can remove the bananas from the airfryer.

7. Serve with your choice of topping - ice-cream, creme fraiche, custard, whipped cream etc.

Apple and Mixed Berry Crumble

Prep time: 15 mins

Cook time: 15 - 20 mins

Serves: 4

Ingredients:

Fruit Base

- 300 g apples
- 150 g mixed berries (frozen berries will work too)
- 50 g brown sugar
- 1 tsp cinnamon

Crumble

- 200 g plain flour
- 100 g butter (soft)
- 70 g light brown sugar
- 50 g oats

Served with cream, ice cream or custard.

Preparation Instructions:

1. Peel apples and dice very finely.
2. Mix berries, apple slices, sugar and cinnamon together.
3. Put the berry mix into your dish.
4. In a separate bowl, rub the flour and butter together until they have a crumbly texture.
5. Thoroughly mix the sugar and oats into this mixture.
6. Spoon the crumble over the berry and apple.
7. Place the dish in the air fryer at 180°C for about 15 - 20 minutes. The crumble topping should have a golden glow to it.
8. Serve with a choice of cream, ice cream or custard.

Scones

Prep time: 10 mins

Cook time: 15 - 20 mins

Serves: 5

Ingredients:

- 250 g self-raising flour
- 120 ml 7-up / sprite
- 120 ml whipping cream
- 50 g caster sugar
- To glaze: Milk or egg wash.

Preparation Instructions:

1. Sieve flour in a mixing bowl.
2. Add lemonade, sugar and cream.
3. Mix together to combine ingredients. Be careful not to overmix.
4. Dredge some flour on a flat surface and knead the dough.
5. Use a scone cutter to cut individual scones.
6. Place scones in the air fryer basket with a 2 cm space between them.
7. Glaze scones with milk or egg wash and cook at 180°C for 15 - 20 mins.
8. Once the tops are golden, place scones on a wire cooling rack to cool.

Banana Bread

Prep time: 10 mins
Cook time: 30 mins
Serves: 8

Ingredients:

- 95 g self -raising flour
- 2 eggs
- ½ tsp salt
- 60 ml milk
- 1 tsp cinnamon
- 2 bananas
- 95 g sugar
- ½ tsp baking soda
- 1 tablespoon vegetable oil

Preparation Instructions:

1. Mix flour, cinnamon, salt and baking soda in a mixing bowl.
2. Preheat air fryer to 160°C
3. In a separate bowl, mix together bananas, egg, milk, sugar and oil.
4. Slowly, fold wet mixture into dry mixture until all is combined.
5. Pour mixture into a greased cake tin.
6. Place tin in the airfryer and cook for about 30 minutes.
7. After cooking, place bread on a wire rack to cool.

Toffee Popcorn

Prep time: 5 mins
Cook time: 10 mins
Serves: 2

Ingredients:

- 60 g popcorn kernels
- 90 g butter
- 160 g light brown sugar

Preparation Instructions:

1. Preheat the airfryer to 200°C.
2. Put the corn kernels in the airfryer basket and cook for about 5 minutes (or until kernels stop popping)
3. Pour popped corn kernels on a baking tray.
4. Melt the butter over a low heat.
5. Once melted, stir in brown sugar.
6. Pour mixture over popcorn.
7. Toffee popcorn is ready!

Flapjacks

Prep time: 5 mins
Cook time: 20 mins
Serves: 4

Ingredients:

- 100 g butter
- 100 g brown sugar
- 250 g porridge oats
- 2 tbsp honey

Preparation Instructions:

1. Chop butter into pieces and put it in the airfryer to melt at 180°C. (1-2 minutes)
2. Mix the porridge oats, sugar and honey together in a separate bowl.
3. Add the oat mixture to the butter pan and mix well.
4. Cook at a reduced temperature of 160°C for 12 -15 minutes.

Shortbread

Prep time: 10 mins
Additional setting time: 1- 2 hours
Cook time: 8 - 10 mins
Serves: 5

Ingredients:

- 85 g butter
- 30 g icing sugar
- 95 g plain flour

Preparation Instructions:

1. Beat butter and sugar together until the two are incorporated.
2. Add flour and gently mix. Be careful not to overmix.
3. Form a ball from the dough.
4. Wrap the ball in cling film and place in the fridge for 1 -2 hours.
5. When ready, take dough from the fridge and slice into 1 cm disks.
6. Line the air fryer basket with greaseproof paper.
7. Place shortbread discs in a lined airfryer basket.
8. Leave plenty of space between each disk.
9. Cook at 170°C for 8 - 10 mins.
10. After cooling in the air fryer basket for at least 5 minutes, place biscuits on a wire cooling rack to further cool.

Rich chocolatey custard

Prep time: 15 mins
Cook time: 10 mins
Serves: 2

Ingredients:

- 180 g whipping cream
- 2 egg yolks
- 50 g caster sugar
- 65 g dark chocolate
- ⅛ teaspoon salt
- ⅛ teaspoon vanilla extract

Preparation Instructions:

1. Whisk sugar, egg yolks, salt and vanilla in a mixing bowl.

2.Chop dark chocolate into chip sized pieces.

3.Bring the cream to a low simmer over a medium heat for 3-4 minutes.

4.Slowly, add egg yolk mix to the cream, constantly stirring to combine.

5.Add the chocolate to the pan and continue to heat until chocolate has melted.

6.Preheat the air fryer for 2 minutes.

7.Pour the chocolate mix into two ramekins.

8.Put the ramekins in the pre heated air fryer and cook for 7 minutes.

9.Allow custard to cool on a wire rack for 20 minutes.

10.Cool custard in fridge.

Chocolate Cake

Prep time: 10 mins

Cook time: 45 - 50 mins

Serves: 4

Ingredients:

- 70 g whipping cream
- 3 large eggs
- 120 g caster sugar
- 100 g self-raising flour
- 30 g cocoa powder
- 60 ml sunflower oil
- 40 g chopped walnuts

Preparation Instructions:

1.Preheat the air fryer to 200°C.

2.Mix the flour, eggs, sugar, cocoa powder, cream and oil in a mixing bowl.

3.Use a hand blender on a medium speed to mix the ingredients together.

4.Fold in walnuts to mix.

5.Line a cake tin with greaseproof paper.

6.Pour the batter into the lined tin.

7.Cover with tin foil and add to air fryer.

8.Reduce temperature to 180°C and cook for 45 minutes.

9.Cook until a knife comes out clean and clear from the centre of the cake.

10.Cool on a wire rack before serving.

Cinnamon Roasted Almonds

Prep time: 5 mins

Cook time: 8 mins

Serves: 4

Ingredients:

- ½ teaspoon cinnamon
- 1 tablespoon sugar
- 30 g butter
- 130 g whole almonds

Preparation Instructions:

1. Melt butter in microwave or over a low heat.
2. Add almonds, sugar and cinnamon to the butter and mix well ensuring all nuts are well coated.
3. Arrange almonds in air fryer basket so none are overlapping.
4. Place in an air fryer at 200°C for 4 minutes.
5. After 4 minutes stir almonds and put them back in air fryer for another 4 minutes.
6. Allow to cool before eating.

Chocolate Cheesecake

Prep time: 10 mins

Cook time: 20 mins

Serves: 8

Ingredients:

- 230 g cream cheese
- 100 g crushed digestive biscuits
- 75 g sugar
- 1 teaspoon vanilla extract
- 45 g soft butter
- 2 eggs
- 200 g melted chocolate
- 1 tablespoon flour

Preparation Instructions:

1. Melt the butter over a low heat.
2. Once melted, add the biscuit crumbs and mix well.
3. Press the buttered biscuit crumb into the bottom of a springform tin.
4. Set in fridge / freezer while preparing the rest of the recipe.
5. In a mixing bowl, mix cream cheese and sugar.
6. Beat in eggs one at a time.
7. Add flour and vanilla extract to the filling mixture.
8. Slowly pour melted chocolate into the filling mixture.
9. Stirring all the time to evenly distribute the chocolate.
10. Spoon filling over biscuit base.
11. Bake for 15 - 20 minutes in an air fryer at 220°C.

12.Cool and refrigerate until cheesecake is fully set.

Dried Strawberries

Prep time: < 5 mins
Cook time: 1 hour
Serves: 3

Ingredients:

- 200 g fresh strawberries

Preparation Instructions:

1.Preheat the air fryer to the lowest possible setting.
2.Remove stems and slice strawberries very thinly.
3.Arrange strawberry slices in air fryer basket.
4.Cook for one hour at 90°C, turning them at the 30 minute mark.

Deep-Fried (Air-fried) Oreos

Prep time: 5 mins
Cook time: 10 mins
Serves: 6

Ingredients:

- 50 g plain flour
- 150 ml milk
- One egg
- 1 tsp oil
- 6 oreos
- Icing sugar to sprinkle

Preparation Instructions:

1.To make pancake batter, mix flour, milk, sugar and oil in a bowl.
2.Whisk until the batter is smooth.
3.Preheat air fryer to 180°C.
4.Dip each oreo in the pancake batter and place in airfryer basket. Keep a small gap between each oreo in the air fryer basket.
5.Cook for 5 minutes, flip them around and then cook for a further 2 minutes until golden.
6.Dust cooked oreos with some icing sugar.

Granola

Prep time: 5 mins
Cook time: 25 mins
Serves: Approx 150 g

Ingredients:

- 115 g rolled oats
- 60 g nut butter of choice
- ½ tsp cinnamon
- ½ tsp vanilla extract
- Choice of dehydrated fruits
- 30 g melted coconut oil
- 90 g honey
- 30 g chopped nuts
- 10 g shredded coconut

Preparation Instructions:

1. Preheat air fryer to 135°C.
2. In a large mixing bowl, combine all your ingredients.
3. Line the air fryer basket with greaseproof paper.
4. Transfer the granola mixture to the lined basket, ensuring there is a thin layer of granola.
5. Put in air fryer for 20-25 minutes.
6. Allow to cool in basket before transferring.

16" Five Cheese Pizza

Prep time: 8 minutes
Cook time: 16-20 minutes
Serves 6
Pizza has been a family favourite since I could remember. Our air fryer recipe contains all 5 cheeses which really impacts the flavour and texture.

Ingredients

- 16" worth of dough
- 50g mozzarella cheese
- 50g parmesan cheese
- 50g Romano cheese
- 6 tbsp tomato sauce
- 50g cheddar cheese
- 50g asiago cheese
- 2 ½ tbsp olive oil

Preparation Instructions

1. Preheat the air fryer at 200°C for 4-5 minutes
2. Roll out the dough and place it on two 8" pizza pan
3. Top the dough with tomato sauce and equally divide the cheeses on both pizza doughs
4. Place the pizza into the air fryer at 190°C for 8-10 minutes
5. Remove the pizza and cover with a layer if foil to keep it warm
6. Repeat the process with the other pizza
7. Slice each pizza by 6 slices and serve (2 slices per person)

Family Roast Chicken

Prep time: 5 minutes
Cook time: 95 minutes
Serves 6
Roast chicken is a great main for a family meal. Roast chicken is full of nutrients and flavour. It can be served with a carbohydrate source such as Roast potatoes and/or vegetables.

Ingredients

- 1 large whole chickens (2.2-2.5kg)
- 50ml olive oil
- 10g paprika
- 2 tsp sea salt
- ¼ tsp ground black pepper

- 1 lemon
- 2 Branches of thyme

Preparation Instructions

1. Preheat the air fryer to 180°C
2. Rub the olive oil, paprika, salt and pepper into the chicken
3. Make small incisions into the around the lemon using a knife and insert it into the chicken cavity
4. Similarly, insert the thyme into the cavity of the chicken
5. Gently place the chicken in the barrel if the air fryer at 190°C for 55 minutes ±5-10 Minutes
6. Retrieve the chicken and cut it to preference before serving

Quiche Lorraine

Prep time: 20 minutes

Cook time: 40 minutes

Serves 4

Scones are a family favourite in Britain, eaten during afternoon tea, with a variety of other cakes, biscuits and hot English tea.

Ingredients

- 1 sheet frozen puff pastry
- 175g boneless bacon strips
- 5 large eggs
- 125ml whole milk
- ¼ tsp ground black pepper
- 30ml olive oil
- 130g finely diced onion
- 125ml double cream
- 100g grated Swiss-style

Preparation Instructions

1. Preheat the air fryer at 180° for 5 minutes
2. Meanwhile, line a 4"x18" tart tin with puff pastry (detachable base tin)
3. Layer the pastry with baking paper
4. Place the tin in the air fryer and cook for 7 minutes at 180°C
5. Remove the baking paper
6. Make light incisions in the paste with a fork
7. Return to air fryer to cook for another 5-6 minutes, then set the pastry aside
8. Place a large pan on a medium heated stove and add oil and bacon for 4-5 minutes
9. Toss in the onions and continue cooking for another 4-5 minutes
10. Once the food content is crisp and golden, set aside
11. Using a stand mixer, whisk eggs, cream, milk, and black pepper
12. Scrape the into the base of the pastry
13. Dash cheese on top of the pastry

14. Pour the creamy egg content on top of the cheese
15. Place the food content back into the air fryer at 160°C for 30 minutes
16. Retrieve the Quiche and set aside to cool
17. Cut into 4 quarters, or 6 pieces if you have a larger family

Family Size Hash Browns and Eggs

Prep time: 5 minutes
Cook time: 30 minutes
Serves 4-5
We could've categorised this recipe as a breakfast, but it is also considered as a British family favourite.

Ingredients

For hash browns
- 500g frozen hash brown potato's
- ½ tsp garlic powder
- 1/8 tsp sea salt
- 1/8 tsp ground black pepper
- 1cal avocado fry spray

For eggs
- 5 large eggs
- ¼ tsp sea salt
- ¼ tsp ground black pepper
- 1cal avocado fry spray

Preparation Instructions

1. Preheat the air fryer at 180°C for 4-5 minutes
2. Generously fry spray the barrel of the air fryer
3. Toss the hash brown in the air fryer
4. Dash the garlic powder, salt and pepper on top
5. Reset the air fryer for 20 minutes
6. Flip and break up the hash browns, then cook for another 5 minutes
7. Remove and set hash brown and set them on the dinner table
8. Generously spray a 6" pizza pan
9. Crack the eggs into the pizza pan, ensuring that you do not break the yolk
10. Place them in the air fryer and cook at 190°C for 4-5 minutes
11. Retrieve the eggs and plate them up
12. Season the eggs
13. Place the eggs on the dinner table and allow and serve

Lunch Time Grilled Cheese Sandwiches

Prep time: 5 minutes

Cook time: 8 minutes

Serves 5

We have given one of the easiest and simplest recipes you will ever come across. The grilled cheese sandwich is perfect for a Sunday afternoon, when everyone is likely to be at home for lunch.

Ingredients

- 10 slices of bread
- 5 thick slices of extra mature British cheddar cheese
- 5 tbsp Worchester sauce

Preparation Instructions

1. Preheat the air fryer at 180°C for 3-4 minutes
2. Meanwhile, drizzle Worchester sauce over the slices of bread
3. Sandwich the cheese in-between the bread and place it in the air fryer
4. Either use the 'grill' setting for 8 minutes, or set the air fryer at 180° for 8 minutes
5. Retrieve the grilled cheese sandwiches and serve

Family Bucket (Air Fried Chicken)

Prep time: 10 minutes

Cook time: 30 minutes

Serves 5

The family bucket has become a favourite in the UK within the last few decades. This recipe is a healthier variant of the K.F.C.

Ingredients

- 1.4kg of different chicken pieces (drum sticks, thighs, breasts)
- 350ml buttermilk
- 240g all-purpose flour
- 2 tsp garlic powder
- 2 tsp salt
- 1cal olive oil spray
- 2 large eggs
- 3 tsp paprika
- 2 tsp onion powder
- 1 tsp ground black pepper

Preparation Instructions

1. Preheat the air fryer at 180°C for 3-4 minutes
2. Amalgamate the buttermilk and eggs in a stand mixer
3. Using a small bowl, combine all of the dry ingredients to make the coating flour

4. Employing some kitchen tongs, submerge each chicken piece in the flour, followed by the buttermilk, then back into the flour
5. Place the chicken in the air fryer and cover it with the fry spray
6. Preferably select the 'air crisp' function or cook the chicken at 180°C for 20 minutes
7. Shake the chicken and cook for another 5 minutes
8. Retrieve the chicken place into a large bowl, then serve

Aracini Rice Balls

Prep time: 30 minutes
Cook time: 30 minutes
Serves 8
Aracho rice balls are one of the more difficult recipes to collate, but they are very tasty and serve as a great starter or side to a main meal.

Ingredients

- 830ml chicken stock
- 40g finely chopped onions
- 45g parmesan cheese
- ½ tbsp chopped basil
- 1/8 sea salt
- 70g flour
- 113g Italian bread crumbs

- 45g butter
- 210g Arborio rice
- 80ml double cream
- 1/8 ground black pepper
- 110g mozzarella cubes
- 3 eggs

Preparation Instructions

1. Start by pouring the chicken stock into the air fryer, preferably using he 'sear/sauté' function for 5 minutes
2. Remove the chicken stock from the air fryer and set aside for later
3. Toss the butter into the air fryer using the same air fryer function
4. Add the onions, followed by the rice
5. Add a quarter of the chicken stock at 2 minute intervals and stir
6. Turn off the air fryer and toss in the double cream, basil, and parmesan. This process forms the risotto
7. Retrieve and spread the risotto on a dish and store it in the refrigerator for 40-50 minutes
8. Spread an egg onto the risotto
9. Hand roll the risotto into 24 small ball, and Submerge a chunk of mozzarella in the centre
10. Prepare 3 bowls
11. In the first bowl, beat 2 eggs
12. In the second bowl, pour flour
13. In the third bowl pour the bread crumbs
14. Dip the rice balls in flour, egg, and then bread crumbs

15. Repeat the process with all of the rice balls
16. Place the rice balls in the air fryer at 200°C for 13 minutes
17. Remove the Arachi rice balls and serve

Toasted Hot Cross Buns

Prep time: 3 minutes

Cook time: 3 minutes

Serves 6

A nice and easy recipe, simply margarine the Buns and toast them using the air fryer. These Buns are a UK family favourite snack, or perfect in a lunch box. Hot Cross Buns are an amalgamation of sweet and savoury as they contain wheat, raisins and sugar.

Ingredients

- 6 Hot Cross Buns
- 6 tsp margarine

Preparation Instructions

1. Cut the nuns horizontally to form to pieces
2. Apply 1 tsp of margarine
3. Place the hot cross buns in the air fryer at 200°C for 4 minutes
4. Remove the Buns and plate them up to serve

Grilled Chicken Breast With Rosemary

Prep time: 10 minutes

Cook time: 17 minutes

Serves 6

A simple and delicious grilled chicken breast seasoned just how we like it in England. This grilled chicken is a stable protein source for families in the UK. This grilled chicken breast can be served with a side of your choice including; rice, vegetables, mash potato etc. Without a doubt, a true family favourite.

Ingredients

- 3 large chicken breasts
- 6 Stalks of rosemary
- 1 tsp garlic powder
- ¼ tsp sea salt

- 1 tbsp olive oil
- 1 ½ tsp paprika
- ¼ tsp onion powder
- ¼ tsp ground black pepper

Preparation Instructions

1. Preheat the air fryer at 180°C for 4-5 minutes
2. Meanwhile, mix all of the dry ingredients into a small bowl using a fork
3. Place the chicken in-between parchment paper and pound the it with a mallet to even out the thickness
4. Rub the dry ingredients into the chicken breast thoroughly
5. Place the chicken in the air fryer and increase the heat to 200°C for 8-10 minutes
6. Flip the chicken and cook for another 8-10 minutes
7. Retrieve the chicken breast, plate it up and with a stalk of rosemary, then serve with your preferred sides

Yorkshire Pudding

Prep time: 10 minutes
Cook time: 17 minutes
Serves 6 (recipe scalable)

Yorkshire puddings were invested in Northern England around the 18th century. They have got to to be one of the top 5 family favourites sides across the UK. Typically Yorkshire puddings are eaten as a side along with food sources like gravy, mash potato, roasts etc.

Ingredients

- 1 Large Egg
- 180g of all-purpose flour
- 180ml milk
- 180ml water
- ¾ tsp table salt

Preparation Instructions

1. You will need to pre prepare the Yorkshire Pudding ingredients by mixing all if the ingredients, and placing them into the refrigerator for 1hr
2. Preheat air fryer to 200°C for 6 minutes
3. Pour 1 tbsp olive oil into the empty ramekins, then place them in the air fryer for 4-5 minutes at 200°C
4. Pour the Pudding mixture into the ramekins and allow them to cook for 18 minutes at the same temperature
5. Retrieve the Yorkshire puddings and serve them as part of a Sunday roast

British Gravy

Prep time: 5 minutes
Cook time: 10 minutes
Serves 6-9

Gravy was invented in the early 20th century. It is a typical British sauce that has become a family favourite served at dinners and most Sunday roasts, as it is perfect on top of meats, chicken Yorkshire puddings, vegetables etc.

Ingredients

- 300-400ml beef stock
- 300-400ml chicken stock
- 55g butter
- 35g flour
- ½ tsp onion powder

Preparation Instructions

1. Use the 'sear/saute' function on the fryer at a medium heat, if applicable (or 180°C)
2. Once the butter is melted, add flour and onion powder, then stir it with a wooden spoon
3. Leave the ingredients for 3 minutes
4. Every 30-40 seconds, pour in a ¼ cup of the beef/chicken stock
5. Within a few minutes, thick gravy should begin to appear
6. Pour the gravy into creamer or pouring mugs be used for dinner

British Scones With Strawberries & Cream

Prep time: 10 minutes
Cook time: 7 minutes
Serves 6
Scones are a family favourite in Britain, eaten during afternoon tea, with a variety of other cakes, biscuits and hot English tea.

Ingredients

- 220g self-raising flour
- 30g golden caster sugar
- 1 beaten egg
- whipped cream
- 90g strawberry Jam
- 55g unsalted butter (cubed)
- 60ml whole milk
- 1cal olive oil fry spray
- 12 fresh strawberries halves

Preparation Instructions

1. Using a medium sized bowl, pour flour, sugar and toss in the cubed butter
2. Hand mix the ingredients to form a crumb like texture
3. Add the milk and roll the dough (1.5-2cm thick)
4. Employing a cutter, shape the dough into 6 Scones
5. Spray the barrel of the air fryer thoroughly
6. Place the scones in the air fryer and brush over them with the beaten egg
7. Air fry the scones at 180°C for 7 minutes

8.Retrieve the scones and cut them horizontally to form 2 halves

9.At the bottom layer apply 15g of Jam, followed by 2 halves of strawberry

10.Dollop whipped cream on top of the strawberries

11.Sandwich the condiments with the top layer of the scones, then serve

Apple Pie

Prep time: 5 minutes

Cook time: 20 minutes

Serves 6

Apple pie originated in England. it was first recorded in 1381. The pie has a sweet and saucy apple filling with layers of crispy pie crust.

Ingredients

- Pre Made Pie crust x2
- 600g apple pie filling
- 1 tbsp unsalted butter
- 1 tsp white sugar
- 1 tsp cinnamon
- 1 tsp brown caster sugar

Preparation Instructions

1.Preheat the air fryer at 180°C for 4-5 minutes

2.Meanwhile, flatten the pie crusts if required

3.Place a crust on the pie pan

4.Evenly pour the apple filling from the can straight onto the pie crust

5.Add the second layer of crust over the apple pie

6.Trim and press down on the edges to seal the pie

7.Make 3 incisions on the centre of the pie using a bread knife. This ensures steam can be released during the cooking process

8.Brush the melted butter over the crust of the pie

9.Sprinkle the sugar and cinnamon over the pie

10.Insert the pie in the air fryer and set the temperature to 210°C for 20-25 minutes

11.Retrieve the golden coloured pie and dust the caster sugar on top

12.Cut 6 slices for the family to enjoy as a dessert

Sage & Onion Stuffing Balls

Prep time: 5 minutes

Cook time: 10-12 minutes

Serves 4

Sage & onion stuffing balls make the perfect savoury addition to dinner or a Sunday roast, with roast chicken, potatoes, veg, Yorkshire puddings and gravy.

Ingredients

- 170g Sage & Onion Stuffing Mix
- 1cal olive oil fry spray
- 425ml Boiling water

Preparation Instructions

1. Preheat the air fryer to 180°C for 10 minutes
2. Meanwhile, add the stuffing mix into a large bowl
3. Pour the boiling water into the stuffing mix, and stir thoroughly using a fork
4. Leave the mixture for 7-8 minutes to set
5. Using the mixture, hand mould 12 equally sized stuffing balls
6. Spray the balls and place them in the air dryer
7. Reset the air fryer to 180°C for 5-6 minutes
8. Utilising kitchen tong, turn the stuffing balls and cook for a further 2-3 minutes
9. Retrieve the crispy stuffing balls and serve with dinner

Apple Sauce

Prep time: 5 minutes

Cook time: 20 minutes

Serves 3-4

British apple sauce is a condiments that is usually served with dinner or a Sunday roast. The sour/sweetness of the apple sauce, adds contrast to savoury dinner.

Ingredients

- 500g cooking apples
- ½ tsp lemon juice
- 1/8 tsp cinnamon
- ½ tsp brown sugar
- 65ml water

Preparation Instructions

1. Place a cake pan in the air fryer and preheat it to 200°C for 3-4 minutes
2. Meanwhile, peel and dice the apples, ensuring that you remove the core
3. Toss the apple pieces into the cake pan and pour over hot water
4. Stir the apples and water to combine
5. Layer the top of the pan with foil and place it back in the air fryer

6. Set the temperature to 180°C and cook the apples for 25 minutes

7. Receive the cooked apples and stir with a wooden spoon to form a sauce

8. Set the apple sauce aside to cool, then serve

Tandoori Chicken thighs

Prep time: 30 minutes

Cook time: 20 minutes

Serves 8

The thigh of the chicken is unique in texture and flavour compared to other cuts like drumsticks, breasts, and wings. Tandoori Chicken has become a British love affair and quite possibly an occasional family favourite.

Ingredients

- 2kg chicken thighs
- 80ml of lemon juice (2 medium lemons)
- 500g of plain low fat Greek yogurt
- 4 tbsp tandoori mix
- ¼ tsp of sea salt
- 1cal olive oil fry spray
- 50g finely diced coriander

Preparation Instructions

1. Using a sharp knife, create 3 small 1/2" incisions horizontally on the flesh of the chicken thigh a

2. Place the chicken thighs into a large bowl and add the sea salt and lemon juice

3. Massage these ingredients onto the chicken and create the first coating

4. In a stand mixer, add Greek yogurt and the tandoori mix

5. Whisk these ingredients until they combine and form a thick orange coloured tandoori marinade

6. Pour the tandoori marinade onto the chicken drum thighs, massaging around the flesh.

7. Cover the bowl with clingfilm and place it in the refrigerator overnight, allowing the flavours to infuse with the chicken

8. Spay the 1cal fry spray around the barrel of your air fryer

9. Preheat the air fryer at 180°C for 4-5 minutes

10. Using some cooking tongs, place the chicken thighs into the barrel of the air fryer and set it to the 'bake/roast' setting at 200°C (if applicable)

11. Leave the chicken drumsticks in the air fryer for around 20 minutes

12. Retrieve the chicken and place them into a large dish

13. Dash the coriander on top of the chicken and set on the dinner table to serve for the family

MEASUREMENT CONVERSION CHART

VOLUME EQUIVALENTS(DRY)

US STANDARD	METRIC (APPROXIMATE)
1/8 teaspoon	0.5 mL
1/4 teaspoon	1 mL
1/2 teaspoon	2 mL
3/4 teaspoon	4 mL
1 teaspoon	5 mL
1 tablespoon	15 mL
1/4 cup	59 mL
1/2 cup	118 mL
3/4 cup	177 mL
1 cup	235 mL
2 cups	475 mL
3 cups	700 mL
4 cups	1 L

VOLUME EQUIVALENTS(LIQUID)

US STANDARD	US STANDARD (OUNCES)	METRIC (APPROXIMATE)
2 tablespoons	1 fl.oz.	30 mL
1/4 cup	2 fl.oz.	60 mL
1/2 cup	4 fl.oz.	120 mL
1 cup	8 fl.oz.	240 mL
1 1/2 cup	12 fl.oz.	355 mL
2 cups or 1 pint	16 fl.oz.	475 mL
4 cups or 1 quart	32 fl.oz.	1 L
1 gallon	128 fl.oz.	4 L

WEIGHT EQUIVALENTS

US STANDARD	METRIC (APPROXIMATE)
1 ounce	28 g
2 ounces	57 g
5 ounces	142 g
10 ounces	284 g
15 ounces	425 g
16 ounces (1 pound)	455 g
1.5 pounds	680 g
2 pounds	907 g

TEMPERATURES EQUIVALENTS

FAHRENHEIT(F)	CELSIUS(C) (APPROXIMATE)
225 °F	107 °C
250 °F	120 °C
275 °F	135 °C
300 °F	150 °C
325 °F	160 °C
350 °F	180 °C
375 °F	190 °C
400 °F	205 °C
425 °F	220 °C
450 °F	235 °C
475 °F	245 °C
500 °F	260 °C

The Dirty Dozen and Clean Fifteen

The Environmental Working Group (EWG) is a nonprofit, nonpartisan organization dedicated to protecting human health and the environment Its mission is to empower people to live healthier lives in a healthier environment. This organization publishes an annual list of the twelve kinds of produce, in sequence, that have the highest amount of pesticide residue-the Dirty Dozen-as well as a list of the fifteen kinds of produce that have the least amount of pesticide residue-the Clean Fifteen.

THE DIRTY DOZEN

- The 2016 Dirty Dozen includes the following produce. These are considered among the year's most important produce to buy organic:

Strawberries	Spinach
Apples	Tomatoes
Nectarines	Bell peppers
Peaches	Cherry tomatoes
Celery	Cucumbers
Grapes	Kale/collard greens
Cherries	Hot peppers

- *The Dirty Dozen list contains two additional items kale/collard greens and hot peppers-because they tend to contain trace levels of highly hazardous pesticides.*

THE CLEAN FIFTEEN

- The least critical to buy organically are the Clean Fifteen list. The following are on the 2016 list:

Avocados	Papayas
Corn	Kiw
Pineapples	Eggplant
Cabbage	Honeydew
Sweet peas	Grapefruit
Onions	Cantaloupe
Asparagus	Cauliflower
Mangos	

- *Some of the sweet corn sold in the United States are made from genetically engineered (GE) seedstock. Buy organic varieties of these crops to avoid GE produce.*

Printed in Great Britain
by Amazon